Who was Henslow?

ISBN 978-1-0369-2157-6

Dedication

This book is dedicated to Tim, my husband, who never doubts I can do what I set out to do.

Many thanks are due to Mar Del Mar Millan Pita, Herbarium Coordinator, Cambridge University Botanic Garden for her patience and sharing my enthusiasm for the project.

Thank you to Professor Beverley Glover, Director and Professor Sam Brockington, Curator of Cambridge University Botanic Garden for their kind permission to proceed with this project.

Professor John S Parker, Former Director of Cambridge University Botanic Garden thank you. I could not have progressed without your considerable knowledge of John Stevens Henslow and your generosity. I appreciate your help with my early draft – any errors remaining are mine and are by no means your responsibility.

Thank you to all the staff and volunteers at Cambridge Botanic Garden who have helped me, with special mention to Elizabeth Rushden and Richard Price.

Thank you to Cory and Herbarium Librarian Frankie Marsh. Thank you to Dr Edwin Rose, Department of History and Philosophy of Science, University of Cambridge.

Thank you to my friend Dr Jane Fairweather for your hospitality and for introducing me to Nicola Currie, Hitcham Vestry and Lisa Harris, Food Museum . These three have helped immeasurably with the Suffolk part of the story.

Love and thanks to my wonderful boys, Mike, Joe, Paddy, Stanley and George and the wonderful girls Sophie, Beth and Anna. Thank you all for sharing me with Henslow for the last eighteen months.

Contents

INTRODUCTION

If, like me, you are lucky enough to live near Cambridge, in the East of England, you may have heard of Cambridge University Botanic Garden. You may even be one of the 300,000 people who visit each year. However, have you heard of John Stevens Henslow?

I confess it is only recently I begun to understand the importance of this man to Cambridge, Botany and our understanding of the natural world. In my fortunate position as volunteer at Cambridge Botanic Garden I have sought out more information.

I find a common question from visitors and friends is

"Who was Henslow"?

FIGURE 1
JOHN STEVENS HENSLOW AS A YOUNG MAN,
LINO PRINT JACK FAWDRY TATHAM

John Stevens Henslow was appointed Professor of Botany at the University of Cambridge in 1825. It was Henslow's vision that propelled the creation of our current Botanic Garden.

In contrast, it is likely you have heard of his most famous student, Charles Darwin who caused controversy in 1859 by publishing,

'On the Origin of Species.'

There are many books about Darwin and excellent, scholarly biographies of Henslow, but I hope this little book will capture your imagination and inspire you to find out more.

CHAPTER ONE

FIGURE 2
LINO PRINT OF HENSLOW AS A CHILD CARRYING A LARGE PUFF BALL
FUNGUS, JACK FAWDRY TATHAM

Was Henslow a Child Prodigy?

Picture a young boy less than five years of age, with curly brown hair, a large smile lighting up his clear face. He is struggling home with a puff ball almost the same size as him, his dress is trailing in the mud. It is around the turn of the 19th Century.

John Stevens Henslow was born in Frindsbury, near Rochester, Kent on 6th February 1796 to John Prentis Henslow and Frances, daughter of wealthy brewer Thomas Stevens. In keeping with the custom of the time their eldest son was named after his father and his grandfather.

Sir John Henslow (1730-1815) was the Chief Surveyor to the Royal Navy, he was a clever draftsman who became a naval architect. Although he is unlikely to have travelled the world from his base in Chatham, there is a Cape Henslow in Guadalcanal in the Solomon Islands. This reflects the high standing in which Sir John was held in the British Navy.

Photograph of one of the Solomon Islands in the Pacific Ocean

FIGURE 3 (ALAMY STOCK PHOTO)

His son John Prentis Henslow was a capable young solicitor in Enfield. When his principal had an untimely, fatal fall from a horse, John Prentis took over the legal practice in his twenties. We will see similarities when at a similar age, his eldest son John Stevens held two University Chairs by the age of twenty-nine. John Prentis was invited back to Rochester to join the Wine Merchant Business of his uncle and namesake William Prentis. Here the solicitor, turned wine merchant, married Frances Stevens in 1795.

John Prentis invested in his father-in-law's brewery. Thomas Stevens retired from the brewery, building himself the fine house in 1780, Gad's Hill Place (where Charles Dickens would later reside). Our protagonist John Stevens, would visit his maternal grandfather and used the opportunity to explore the surrounding countryside, as evidenced by his natural history collection and notes.

Dickens' Rochester/Chatham

charlesdickenspage.com

© David A Perdue

The Charles Dickens Page

charlesdickenspage.com

- Gad's Hill Place and The Falstaff Pub (1 mile further)

Charles Dickens lived in the seaport town of Chatham in Kent from 1817 to 1823 (aged 5 to 11). He referred to this time as the happiest of his childhood and uses the area as a backdrop for several of his novels. He moved back to the area in 1860, buying Gad's Hill Place where he died in 1870.

- Select an area on the map to find out more about it and how it relates to Dickens

- Dickens' Homes

Gravesend Rd
Strood Hill
Strood
High Street
Frindsbury
Location
Rochester Bridge
Strood Station
Rochester
River Medway
Tidal Area
Chatham Reach
Royal Dock Yard
Tidal Area
St Mary's Church
Royal Dock Yard Perimeter Wall
Chatham
Chatham Lines
The Brook
Mr Giles' School
High Street
Chatham Station
No. 2 Ordnance Terrace
Fort Pitt
Newhroad
Royal High Street
Star Hill
Fort Clarence
St Margaret's St
Maldstone Rd
The Vines
Vines Lane
Crow Lane
High Street
Restoration House
Travellers' Twopenny
Theatre
Pumblechook's
Eastgate House
Minor Canon Row
Rochester Cathedral
Rochester Castle
Durdles' Yard
The Bull Inn
College Gate
Tope's House
Guildhall
Corn Exchange

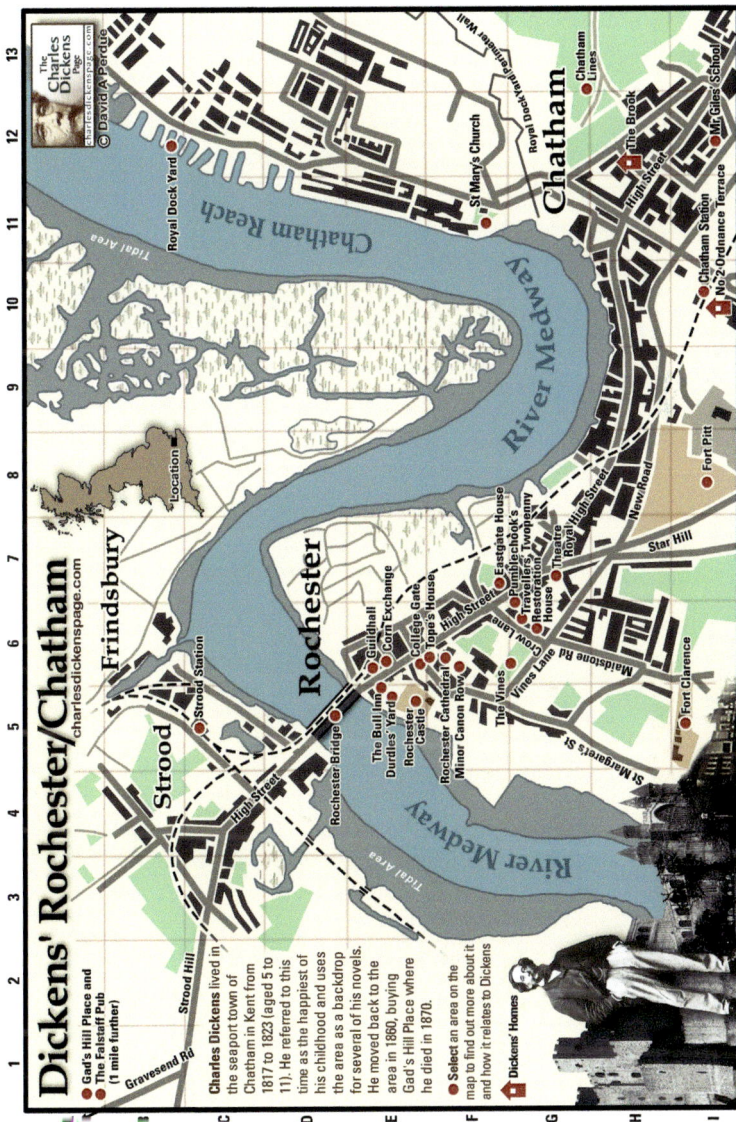

FIGURE 4 DICKENS' ROCHESTER/CHATHAM,
BY KIND PERMISSION OF DAVID A PERDUE

13

In 1808 John Prentis went back to practice law, in St Albans, where he died in 1854, just seven years before his eldest child.

That eldest child John Stevens was the first-born of eleven Henslow children, sadly three of his siblings died in infancy. Henslow appears to have enjoyed a happy childhood, with family outings and holidays enthusing his inquiring mind. From an early age, his interest in the natural world was encouraged by his parents. John Prentis and Frances Henslow were also keen collectors. They tolerated his tendency to get muddy as he explored the countryside. The enormous puffball he collected was displayed in their hall and proudly shown to visitors as a portent of John Stevens' budding talent.

The young Henslow recorded his findings with sketches and watercolours. He entertained his siblings with a model of a caterpillar and made flares by burning phosphorus. From an early age he wanted to share his joy in the natural world.

FIGURE 5
SPHINX LIGUSTRI
(ALAMY STOCK PHOTO)

FIGURE 6 BOAT ON HOO BETWEEN THE THAMES AND MEDWAY RIVERS, KENT (ALAMY STOCK PHOTO)

On family trips he would tirelessly dig in the Medway silt to reveal the molluscs and crustaceans that lurked beneath.

I cannot help but be reminded of Pip and Magwitch in the muddy estuary of Charles Dickens' 'Great Expectations'.

Henslow lived in the same Victorian era when an individual's standing at birth made a considerable difference to that person's prospects.

At the age of nine Henslow went to boarding school in Camberwell. He was befriended by the art teacher George Samuel. The young Henslow was skilled at drawing and shared his teacher's enthusiasm for insects. Samuel introduced John to two notable zoologists of the time. The first being Dr William Elford Leach who was the Assistant Keeper (Curator) at the British Museum. James Francis Stephens, an amateur with the largest known collection of British insects was the second inspirational patron. The young Henslow collected unusual shells and butterflies from the Medway estuary and its salt marshes. Henslow helped Leach catalogue the zoological collections at the British Museum. Corophium longicorne, found by a certain J. Henslow is one of the Museum's crustaceans.

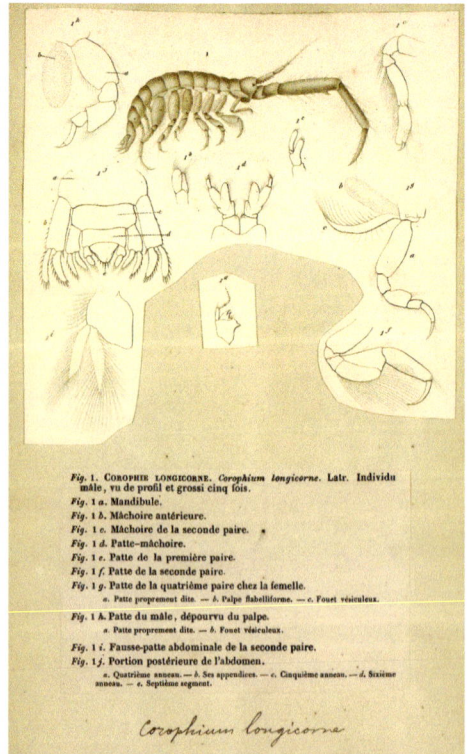

FIGURE 7
COROPHIUM LONGICORNE
(ALAMY STOCK PHOTO)

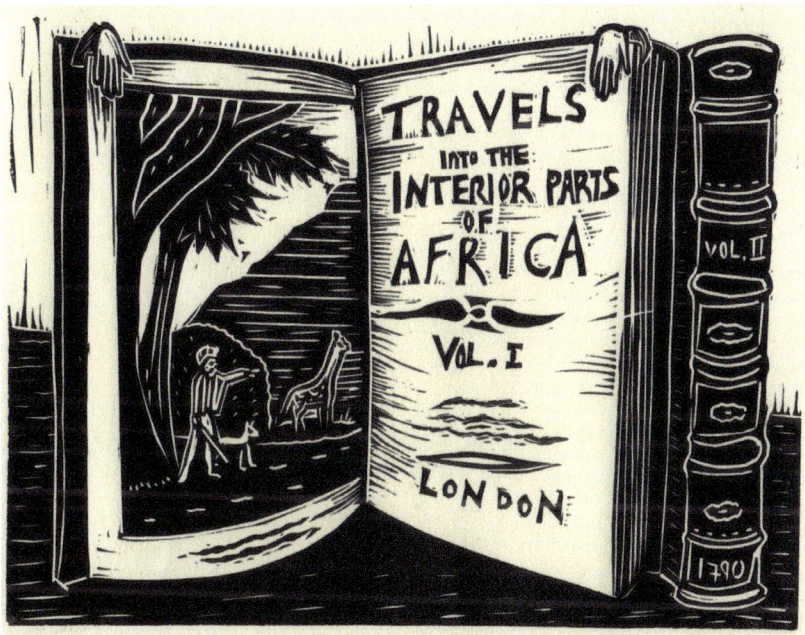

FIGURE 8
LINO PRINT - TRAVELS INTO THE INTERIOR PARTS OF AFRICA,
JACK FAWDRY TATHAM

The book *'Travels into the Interior Parts of Africa'* by Levaillant, was awarded to the fourteen-year-old John as a school prize in 1810. This fired up his enthusiasm to explore the world. It is understandable given the dangers of travelling in the nineteenth century and their recent experiences of child bereavement, John's parents were vehemently against this idea. Leach and Stephens were full of encouragement. Judging by the travel books on his shelves on his death in 1861, it was a dream Henslow could never relinquish.

Leonard Jenyns his biographer and brother-in-law described Henslow as always active and always busy. He appears to be quick to learn, valuing his findings and questioning their significance from a young age. His collecting may have been a common pastime for a 19th child but to me in the 21st Century, his industry, passion and success demonstrated significant talent.

I consider him a child prodigy.

CHAPTER TWO

Was Henslow a Good Student?

In 1814 John Stevens Henslow gained a place at St John's College Cambridge to study mathematics. St John's had been the first college to introduce twice yearly public examinations in 1765.

FIGURE 9
ST JOHN'S COLLEGE,
KATE HOOPER

Henslow was top of his class in the first year and was awarded a scholarship in year two. He was amongst the prize winners in his final year.

He greatly enjoyed attending lectures on chemistry and mineralogy, but these were not part of his final examination or Tripos, so named as the students had to sit on a three-legged stool to take their final examination.

His friends included J.G.Lefevre, the top student or 'Senior Wrangler' of the Final examinations, who later became Clerk to Parliament.

In 1818, Lefevre introduced him to Adam Sedgwick the new Professor of Geology. Henslow attended Sedgwick's lecture and soon mastered the fundamentals of geology.

Sedgwick invited Henslow to join his field trip to the Isle of Wight in 1819. John impressed the professor with his knowledge and acumen.

FIGURE 10
STATUE OF PROFESSOR ADAM SEDGWICK AT THE MUSEUM OF EARTH
SCIENCES NOW NAMED AFTER HIM IN CAMBRIDGE (ALAMY STOCK PHOTO)

FIGURE 11
AMMONITE FOUND BY JOE HOOPER, PHOTOGRAPH TIM HOOPER

A large ammonite similar to this one was collected on the Isle of Wight Trip by Henslow. Henslow's ammonite is held in the Sedgwick Museum in Cambridge. Henslow's proficiency enabled him to lead his own expeditions to other parts of Britain.

After graduating in 1818 Henslow acted as demonstrator for James Cumming, Professor of Chemistry in Cambridge, it appears the phosphorus burning antics of his youth were not wasted.

Henslow was also inspired by Edward Daniel Clarke, Professor of Mineralogy who attracted audiences of up to 200 to his lectures, with tales of his travel supported by fine illustrations.

FIGURE 12
LECTURE ROOMS OF THE BOTANIC GARDEN

Mineralogy and Botany were strongly linked in 19th Century Cambridge. Clarke's popular Mineralogy Course was delivered in Professor Thomas Martyn's lecture theatre in the Botanical Museum.

Clarke being a skilled artist, used his own oil paintings to decorate the lecture room. One painting was a depiction of Mount Vesuvius erupting, this was complimented by a working model made from cork. Clarke was a tough act to follow when Henslow became Professor of Mineralogy in 1822.

FIGURE 13
PHOTOGRAPH OF
MOUNT VESUVIUS,
(ALAMY STOCK PHOTO)

FIGURE 14
POLYBIUS HENSLOWII, LINO PRINT JACK FAWDRY TATHAM

Henslow continued to forward zoological findings to his childhood mentors. It appears they, in turn, held him in high regard. In 1817 Henslow collected a crab from the north coast of Devon, which he sent to Leach. The latter named it Polybius henslowii or Henslow's Swimming Crab.

Dr William Leech and James Stephens proposed their friend and 'zealous student' for the Linnaean Society whilst he was in his final undergraduate year. The Linnaean Society, founded in 1788 was named after the Swedish taxonomist Karl Linnaeus. It is still active and promotes the science of natural history.

Henslow was, elected as Fellow of the Linnean Society on 9th February 1818, three days after his twenty second birthday.

The zoologists followed John's career for many years. William Leach named the sea cucumber Jemania henslowiana, after Henslow sent him a specimen from Aberystwyth in 1819. Leach named new bivalve found at Baits Bite Lock on the River Cam, Cyclas henslowiana. James Stephens described a moth Setina irorella, as collected in Rochester, by Rev Professor John Henslow.

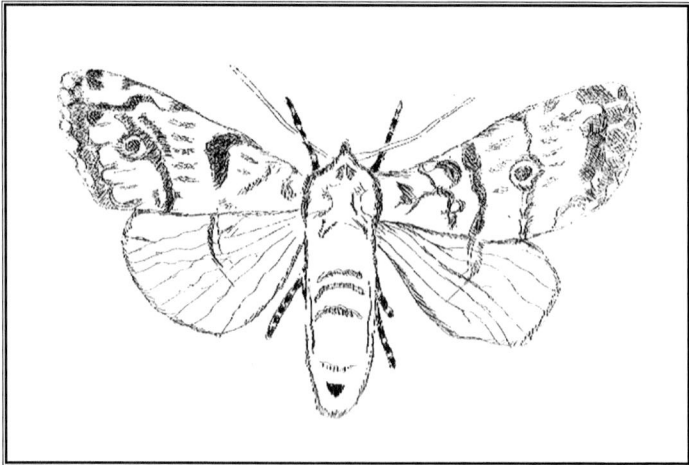

FIGURE 15
SETINA IRORELLA, ETCHING BY KATE HOOPER

Some would debate whether Henslow was a good student. He certainly had natural talent and when applied to subjects he was interested in, the combination of his intellect and hard work bore tremendous results.

Leonard Jenyns his friend and brother-in-law denied he was distracted from mathematics, although he was devoted to natural history

'His powers of reasoning and clear faculties well suited him for studies which necessitated much application of the mind and close thought'.

CHAPTER THREE

Was Henslow a Good Educator?

'He had an untiring zeal to win others over to the
love of pursuits he keenly relished himself'

Jenyns

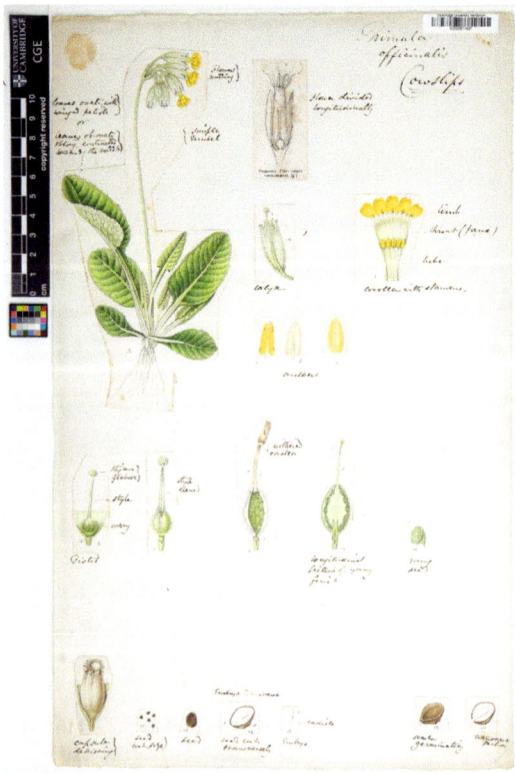

FIGURE 16
EARLY HENSLOW
TEACHING SHEET ON
PRIMULA OFFICINALIS

When tasked with entertaining his younger siblings, John Stevens Henslow took them on nature trips in the Kent countryside that surrounded their family house. He would encourage them to examine their animal, plant and fungal findings thoroughly. His sisters shared his love of drawing.

In 1819 one year after graduating, Henslow organised a trip for students to document the Geology of the Isle of Man. He prepared activities for the students and led by example with his own studies and research.

Professor of Mineralogy, Edward Clarke died in 1822 and despite being just 26 years of age, Henslow was appointed as the new Professor. E.D. Clark had used oil paintings, crystals he had collected and models to demonstrate his Mineralogy Lectures.

Although inspired by Clark's visual aids, Henslow rewrote the Mineralogy syllabus on succeeding his Professorship with his typical diligence and attention to detail. Henslow had studied the work of Abbé René Just Haüy, a French crystallographer who had described crystal structure by mathematical principles in the early 1800s. Haüy assigned newly discovered crystals to mathematically defined families. He postulated that complex crystals were transformations of primitive crystal forms. Henslow published a paper on the crystallisation of gold in the Magazine of Natural History in 1828. His second paper was written in French, indicating the breadth of his education.

Despite his enthusiasm and interest in Mineralogy, Henslow leapt at the opportunity of a new Academic Chair, when Thomas Martyn died in 1825. He had already started his herbarium of British plants despite his lack of formal botanical training.

Thomas Martyn had been in post as Professor of Botany since 1762, when the first Botanic Garden opened in Central Cambridge. He succeeded his father, John who as the second Professor of Botany had been active in medical and economic botany The first Professor, appointed in 1724, was Richard Bradley who had a keen interest in horticulture.

In 1760 Richard Walker the Vice-Master of Trinity College purchased the five-acre plot of land where an Augustinian friary had stood in in the centre of Cambridge. Walker, an enthusiastic gardener, donated this site to the University in trust with his plans for a 'public Botanic Garden', hence this first botanic garden is referred to as the Walkerian Garden.

Walker's vision was
'by making use of the plants grown there, trials and experiments shall be regularly made and repeated, in order to discover their virtues, for the benefit of mankind'.

FIGURE 18 CAMBRIDGE BOTANIC GARDEN 1815 DRAWN BY W WESTALL, ENGRAVED BY J SADLER

Thomas Martyn designed the plant layout in the Botanic Garden, catalogued his father's work and as Professor and as 'Dr Walker's Reader' delivered botany lectures from 1764-1796. Little research was performed during his tenure, but a large plant collection was recorded in 1770. Poor health prevented Thomas Martyn from delivering a single botany lecture in the last 29 years of his 63-year tenure.

FIGURE 19 PROFESSOR THOMAS MARTYN, (ALAMY STOCK PHOTO)

He had tried to resign before he reached his ninth decade, but a suitable (Anglican) successor could not be found.

Charles Miller, Martyn's horticultural advisor, was the son of Philip Miller, Curator of the Apothecaries Society Physic Garden in Chelsea. Not surprisingly the Walkerian Garden resembled the established Chelsea Physic Garden, which can be visited in London today. The education of medical students was the primary use for such a garden.

Candidate List for
Chair of Botany 1825

Rev R Daniel

Rev W Pulling

Rev Garnons

Prof Rev J S Henslow

When Henslow was appointed as Professor of Botany on 17th August 1825 at his own admission he

'knew little about botany but knew as much as any resident in Cambridge'.

Henslow wanted his students to learn botany practically. He provided them with fresh flowers from the Botanic Garden to dissect on wooden plates with scalpels and needles.

Over three months he had created seventy clear watercolour posters sized 20 by 26 inches (51 by 66 cm) to illustrate the parts of flowers and arrangements of leaves. These were large enough to be seen from the opposite side of the lecture room and were accurate enough to be used until the 1960s. E.D. Clark used oil paintings, crystals he had collected and models to accompany his Minerology lectures, but Henslow was the first to give formally illustrated lectures in England.

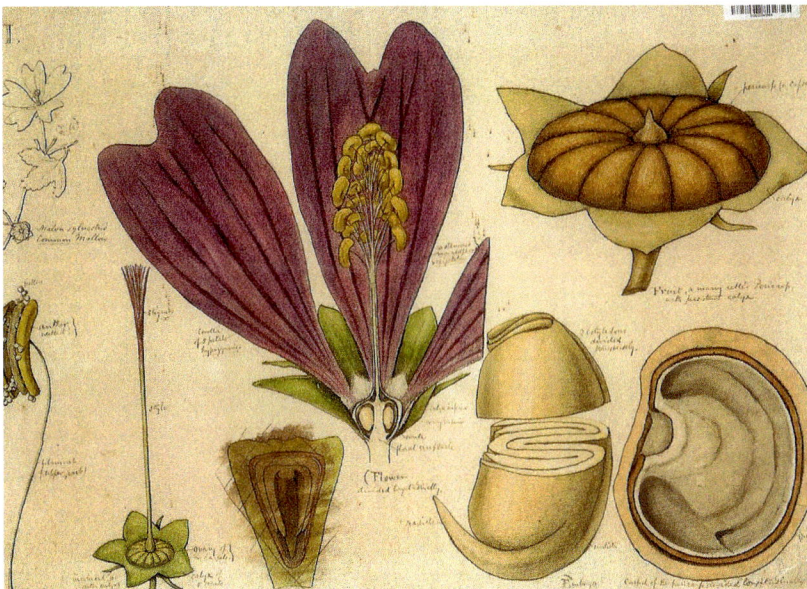

FIGURE 20
BOTANICAL ILLUSTRATION OF MALVACEAE DRAWN BY HENSLOW,
CAMBRIDGE UNIVERSITY HERBARIUM

Henslow's Botany syllabus was published in 1833. He was keen to stress botany was far more than just naming plants. He wanted his students to make their discoveries and understand how the plants worked. Henslow divided his teaching into Demonstrative Botany (Plant Anatomy) with Physiological Botany. These were complemented by Henslow's nature excursions.

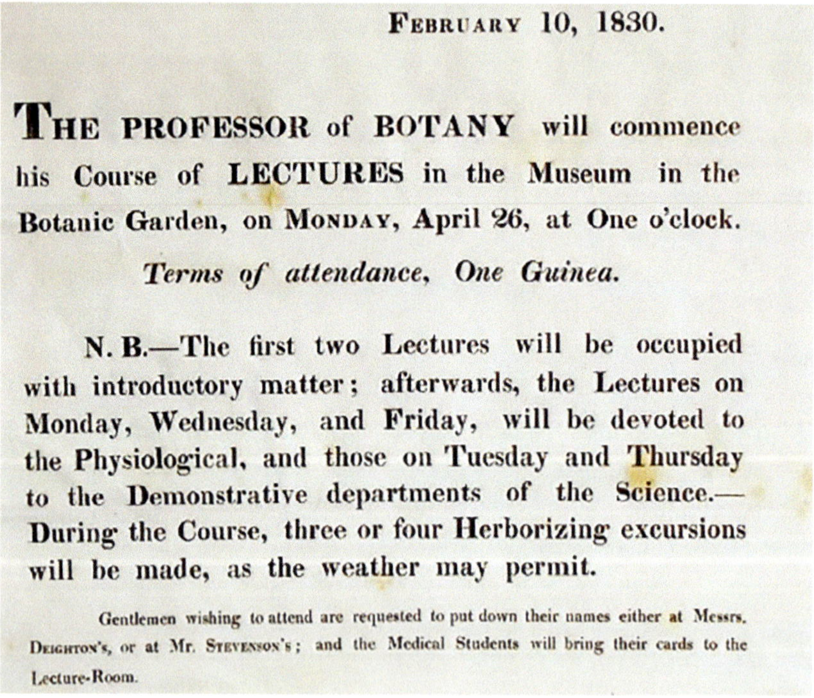

FEBRUARY 10, 1830.

THE PROFESSOR of BOTANY will commence his Course of LECTURES in the Museum in the Botanic Garden, on MONDAY, April 26, at One o'clock.

Terms of attendance, One Guinea.

N. B.—The first two Lectures will be occupied with introductory matter; afterwards, the Lectures on Monday, Wednesday, and Friday, will be devoted to the Physiological, and those on Tuesday and Thursday to the Demonstrative departments of the Science.— During the Course, three or four Herborizing excursions will be made, as the weather may permit.

Gentlemen wishing to attend are requested to put down their names either at Messrs. DEIGHTON's, or at Mr. STEVENSON's; and the Medical Students will bring their cards to the Lecture-Room.

FIGURE 21
ANNOUNCEMENT OF THE BOTANY COURSE 1830,
CAMBRIDGE UNIVERSITY HERBARIUM

The Reading List for Henslow's Botany Students included 'British Flora' by William Hooker and John Lindley's 'Introduction to Botany'.

FIGURE 22
WILLIAM JACKSON HOOKER, PROFESSOR OF BOTANY AT GLASGOW THEN FIRST DIRECTOR OF KEW BOTANIC GARDENS. FATHER OF JOSEPH HOOKER (SON-IN-LAW TO J S HENSLOW). ALAMY STOCK PHOTO

FIGURE 23 JOHN LINDLEY, ASSISTANT SECRETARY TO THE ROYAL
HORTICULTURAL SOCIETY, PROFESSOR OF BOTANY, UNIVERSITY OF
LONDON. ALAMY STOCK PHOTO

Henslow ensured his students had microscopes in order to study
plant anatomy. They were instructed in plant hybridisation,
variation and in plant 'monstrosities' that differed from the
normal type of the species but occurred spontaneously. In
Henslow's time little was known about genetics, he accepted the
Lamarckian view of plasticity in heredity.

Jean–Baptiste Lamarck, proposed that organisms change how
they use structures in response to the environment and these
changes are passed on to their offspring. Gregor Mendel did not
publish his seminal work on the pea plants describing genetic
inheritance until 1866 (five years after Henslow's death). This
would be rediscovered and elaborated on in the twentieth
century when Darwin's theory of evolution became more widely
accepted.

The geographical distribution and the effects of the environment on plant growth was part of the botany course. Excursions such as nature walks, barge trips or coach journeys to explore habitats were extremely popular. Henslow displayed his enthusiasm by pointing out plants, insects, amphibians and fossils along the trail, we are reminded of his trips with his siblings in Kent. Lists of the plants seen were compiled and printed.

One of his students was Joseph Hooker, son of William Hooker. Joseph went on to marry Frances Henslow (John and Harriet's eldest daughter) in 1851. He succeeded his father as Director of Kew in 1865. Joseph Hooker reported as a student of Henslow,

'we used our eyes, hands and heads as well as our books'.

FIGURE 24 JOSEPH HOOKER, ALAMY STOCK PHOTO

After three months they were well prepared for the examinations in the anatomy, physiology and classification of plants.

Erasmus Darwin had told his younger brother Charles about Henslow's entertaining lectures and that he knew every branch of science. The Darwin brothers as schoolboys had set up their own garden laboratory. In a similar way to Henslow entertaining his younger siblings, they had carried out chemical reactions and had grown crystals. Their father was not enthusiastic but let them use the tool shed. Their mother Susannah (née Wedgwood) may have been more encouraging as her family provided the Wedgwood patented fireproof porcelain for their experiments.

Charles Darwin described the day in 1828 when he met Henslow as the luckiest day in his life. It has been said he was transformed from an academic failure to a star pupil by Henslow's inspired teaching. Darwin observed that Henslow,

'had a remarkable power of making the young feel completely at ease with him though we were all awe-struck with the amount of his knowledge. Before I met him, I heard one young man sum up his attainments by simply saying that he knew everything. No man could have been better informed to win the entire confidence of the young and to encourage them in their pursuits.'

Darwin recalled how he had rushed off to tell Henslow he had discovered tubes exserted (protruding) from pollen grains under microscopy. Henslow agreed how interesting this was and its meaning but let him down gently that it was not a new finding. Darwin noted that whereas other professors might have ridiculed, Henslow had instilled in Charles the value of discovering nature for himself.

The new Professor was interested in the geographical distribution of plants and was keen to study the fascinating specimens returned by the plant hunters. Large species such as North American trees were being brought back to the United Kingdom. With the small Walkerian Garden not able to accommodate such species, Henslow's great project began.

He foresaw the need to study plants *'in their own right"*, with specimens clearly labelled and arranged to educate botany students. He needed a garden larger than the five acres of the Walkerian Garden. After much discussion, canvassing and even an Act of Parliament the current site for Cambridge University Botanic Garden was purchased in 1831.

Trinity Hall had farmland just a mile south of the Walkerian Garden, their 40 acres (16 hectares) was chosen. Observant visitors will spot Trinity Hall's coat of arms over the gate to the Botanic Garden on Brookside, commemorating the sale.

FIGURE 25
TRINITY HALL COAT OF ARMS ON
MAIN ENTRANCE GATE, K HOOPER

In 1846 Henslow prepared an

'Address to the Members of the University of Cambridge on the expediency of improving, and on the funds required for remodelling and supporting The Botanic Garden.'

He emphasized the importance of botany as a gateway to zoological research, in addition to being the key to understanding agriculture and horticulture. The discipline of classifying plants, he proposed, would improve the discipline of the students.

Henslow suggested to his colleagues that Cambridge should be keeping pace in the advancement of all sciences. He described how he had visited Kew and consulted the Superintendent Sir William Hooker (formerly Professor of Botany in Glasgow) and Dr John Lindley, (Assistant Secretary to the Royal Horticultural Society and Professor of Botany at the University of London) to discover their teaching methods.

Henslow appealed to Cambridge pride proposing their Botanic Garden

'should at least be on equal footing with those of Edinburgh, Glasgow and Dublin'.

To support his project Henslow was requesting a Curator and further £10,000 to fund the project after sale of the old Botanic Garden site. The Curator appointed was Andrew Murray, previously Curator of Liverpool Botanic Garden. Murray, like Henslow subscribed to De Candolle's system of dividing flowering plants according to their flowering parts. He attended his interview with a plan for the Garden including the Systematic Beds. Murray's design was followed for the most part of what is now known as the Victorian Garden. The Cambridge Systematic Beds are unique in their design and preserve the legacy of Henslow and Murray.

FIGURE 26 CAMBRIDGE UNIVERSITY BOTANIC GARDENS SYSTEMATIC BEDS, HOWARD RICE.

Henslow adapted his undergraduate Botany Course to use in Hitcham Village School (as I will describe further in Chapter Five). Nine diagrams from Henslow's successful school syllabus were produced by the Department of Art and Science and sent to every National School in the country. This was the First National Curriculum in the United Kingdom. Records of his lessons were preserved in the South Kensington Museum. Whilst visiting the museum in London, American Eliza Youmans was inspired to compile her 'First Book of Botany' in 1870. She attributed her schedule to that tried and tested by Prof J. S. Henslow for his 'poor country children', but Youmans simplified the format for her own students.

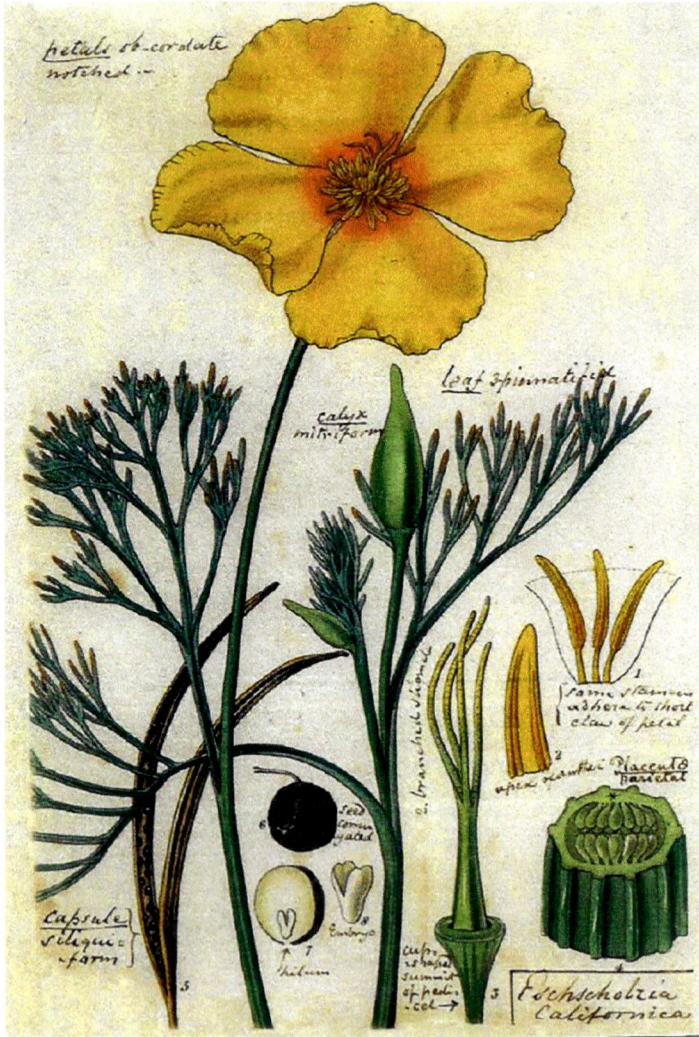

FIGURE 27
ESCHSCHOLZIA CALIFORNICA, WILLIAM JACKSON HOOKER ILLUSTRATION
ANNOTATED BY JOHN STEVENS HENSLOW CGE01967 CAMBRIDGE
UNIVERSITY HERBARIUM

John Stevens Henslow is listed as a Founder member of the Senate of London University in 1836. This was a step forward to broadening University Education beyond Oxford and Cambridge and admitting 'dissenters' as students. Henslow was an examiner at London University from 1838 and he insisted on a practical knowledge of botany. One of Henslow's last official duties was as examiner in botany, in Cambridge in March 1861. The Natural Sciences Tripos had been fully instituted in the University of Cambridge in 1860.

Henslow was invited to teach botany to the children of Queen Victoria and Prince Albert when he was sixty-four. It appears he was introduced through his son-in-law Joseph Hooker. Palace Secretary I.A. Clark writes in April 1860,

"I am very glad to hear from Dr Hooker that you are quite willing to give the Royal Children a few lectures in Botany. Your present course of lectures terminates in May, and that you will be free in June which will be a good month to give lectures. If you will let me know what time in June will suit you and the course best, I will arrange it with the Prince Consort."

FIGURE 28
QUEEN VICTORIA, PRINCE ALBERT AND THEIR CHILDREN
ALAMY STOCK PHOTO

Henslow had a unique gift in being able to observe fine detail but also see the bigger picture. I consider this made him a great educator. In the same way he enjoyed looking down a microscope, he would encourage the youngest child to explore nature. He could summarise the geology of an island and bring about a paradigm shift in lifelong education. He was a great educator.

CHAPTER FOUR

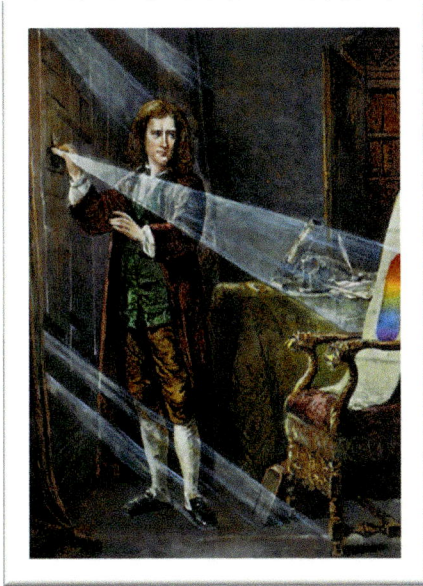

Was Henslow a Good Philosopher (Scientist)?

FIGURE 29
ISAAC NEWTON (ALAMY)

At the beginning of the 19th Century, science in Cambridge was in a stagnant stage. Professors were appointed to departmental chairs but were not expected to undertake their own research or further the understanding of their subjects. Mathematics was taught according to Newton's principles which had been described almost one hundred years previously.

Scientist was a term not used until 1834 when first used by the Cambridge philosopher and friend of Henslow, Prof William Whewell to describe another great scientific mind, Mary Somerville.

Henslow spent the summer of 1819 on the Isle of Man. His visit coincided with the discovery of fossilised bones of an Irish Elk. The local blacksmith was using his knowledge of equine anatomy to reassemble the skeleton. Henslow was impressed when he wrote to Sedgwick

'you know I am not given to the marvellous, but I really think I never saw a more magnificent sight of the kind in my life ... the fellow has really put it together with great ingenuity'

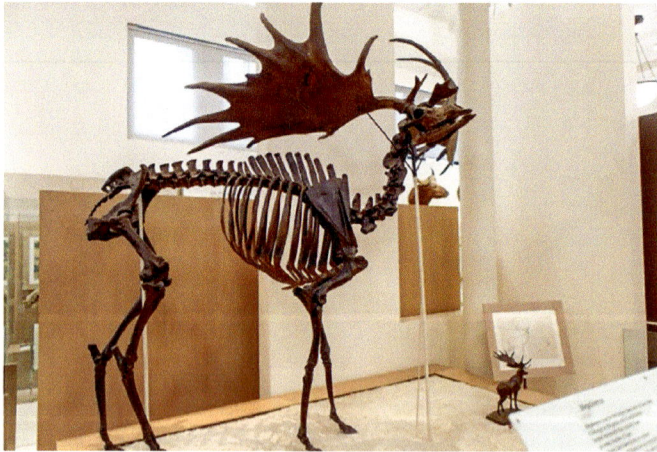

FIGURE 30
FOSSIL OF IRISH ELK, ALAMY STOCK PHOTO

Henslow tried to buy the elk for the Cambridge Collection, but it was claimed by the local Manx Duke who later donated it Edinburgh University.

In 1821 Henslow's first paper was published - a geological survey of the Isle of Man in which he revised the findings of Dr Berger.

Whilst on a field trip to the Isle of Wight, Henslow and Adam Sedgwick shared their excitement for the ancient creatures and plants who had been fossilised in the cliffs. The two of them discussed how they could spread this new knowledge of Geology and Natural History. They decided to form a philosophical society in Cambridge. The two of them wrote to all their friends, including Edward Clark who became a dynamic ally.

The invitation for 12 noon on Tuesday 2nd November 1819, had been signed by 33 people including six heads of colleges, six professors, 11 tutors and a librarian. Henslow's and Sedgwick's hard work in what we today describe as networking, had paid off and a large crowd attended. The meeting was chaired by Addenbrooke's Hospital physician John Haviland and the discussion centred around the aims of the society to promote the new sciences of mineralogy, geology, chemistry, botany and zoology.

There was a unanimous vote in favour, establishing

'The Cambridge Philosophical Society for the advancement of natural philosophy'.

The committee of nine men established the rules and purposes of the group. It was open to all graduates, but members of council were required to have a Master of Arts. Henslow had graduated in 1818 but had not yet achieved his MA so excluded from the Committee, was made Secretary.

Despite the support amongst like-minded scholars, they were not without detractors. Notably Hugh Rose a clergyman who had graduated in 1817 campaigned against the teaching of science in Cambridge. Rose was concerned that the study of 'reason' undermined religious orthodoxy. However, by setting up a society independent of the University for graduates, the meetings would have no direct effect on undergraduate teaching. The senior members would be encouraged to carry out their own research by exchanging ideas. Gradually these activities would be passed down to the next generation to the benefit of the University and the promotion of science. A gentle reshaping of science research had commenced.

FIGURE 31 SHELLS AND FOSSILS, KATE HOOPER

The first major collection in The Philosophical Society's museum was Henslow's set of insects and shells gathered since childhood. He had collected and labelled specimens from around his family home in Kent starting around his family home in Kent, from his school in Camberwell, from Cambridgeshire and then from the Isle of Wight. The Cambridge Philosophical Society exists to this day holding lectures which cover new advances in all branches of science.

Henslow reviewed the Geology of Anglesey in 1820, leading a group of students. The depth of his survey is recorded in his paper with description of the different locations and samples of rocks which were placed in the Woodwardian (Geology) Museum. Henslow produced the first geological survey of any part of the United Kingdom when he published the hand drawn charts and accompanying diagrams. It was presented to the Cambridge Philosophical Society on 26th November 1821, Henslow was Secretary of the Society at that time. The copies were individually hand water coloured and one such copy is reproduced below. The precision and detail recorded are of extremely high standard and evidence his diligence and technical acumen.

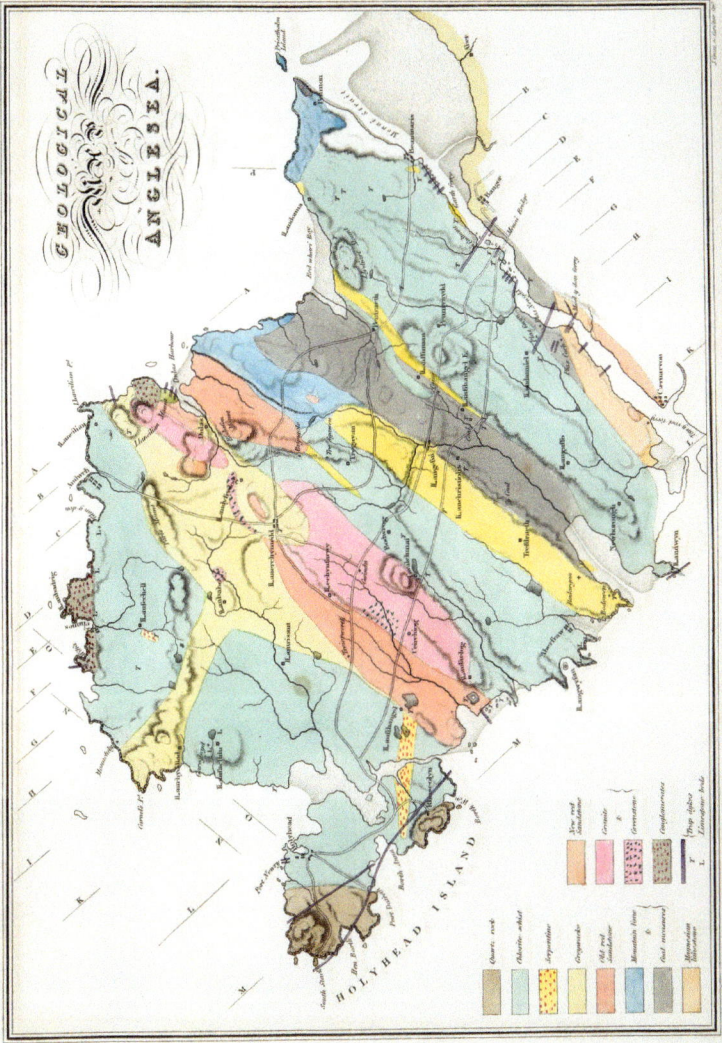

FIGURE 32 GEOLOGICAL SURVEY OF ANGLESEA(Y) BY KIND
PERMISSION OF CAMBRIDGE PHILOSOPHICAL SOCIETY

49

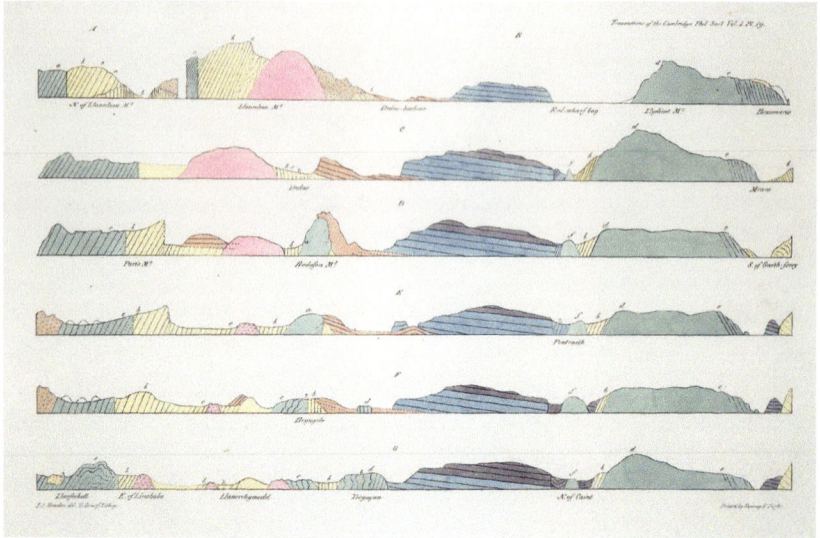

FIGURE 33 AND 34 CROSS SECTIONS

Later in life Henslow returned to study the bed rock. He undertook the first recorded excavations in Rougham in 1843 where the Roman barrows were explored on Eastlow Hill. In 1848 he was a founding vice-president of the Bury St Edmunds and West Suffolk Archaeological Institute. In his inaugural speech Henslow compelled

"Our collections should be viewed as the means of assisting us in the acquisition of real knowledge."

This organisation continues today as the Suffolk Institute of Archaeology and History.

In 1821 however, Henslow began his major research project to collect specimens of every native plant of Britain. He considered the most important question in biology was the nature and limit of species. By 1826 with the help of 200 people, his herbarium contained 15,000 specimens. The plants had been dried, pressed and mounted on card to produce vouchers with examples of 1,200 species. His way of presenting the plants was unique at the time. Being obsessed with variation, Henslow would mount the dried plants from various locations on the same card to illustrate their differences as shown in following the examples.

FIGURE 35
MOENCHIA ERECTA, COLLECTED FROM VARIOUS PLACES, PLANTS AT
SAME MATURITY BUT SHOWING A BELL-SHAPED DISTRIBUTION OF SIZE,
CAMBRIDGE UNIVERSITY HERBARIUM.

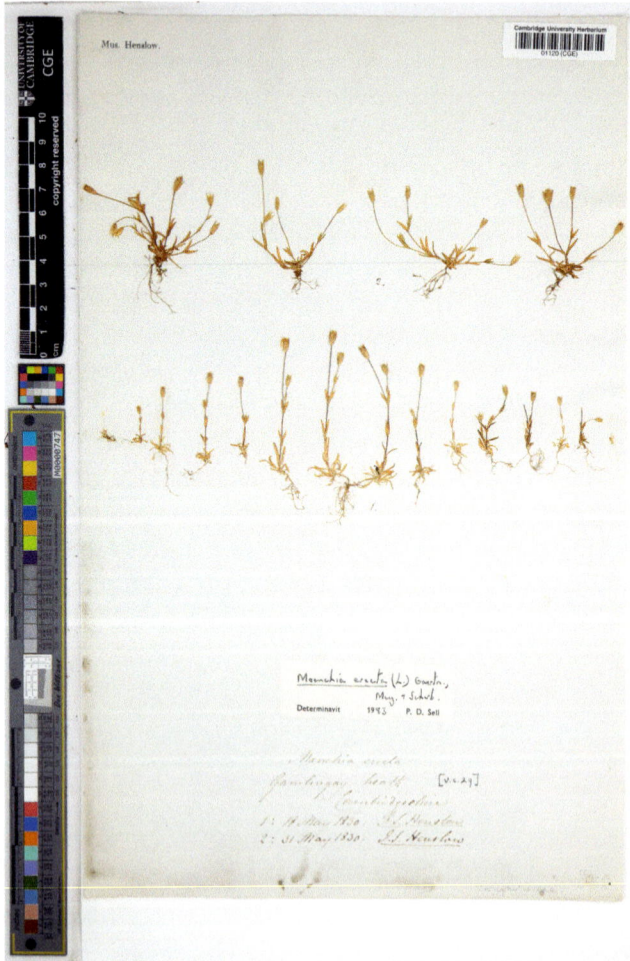

FIGURE 36
JUNCUS TRIGLUMIS (THREE FLOWERED GRASS) SHOWN AS A
COLLATION OF PLANTS SOURCED BY DIFFERENT COLLECTORS
(CAMBRIDGE UNIVERSITY HERBARIUM)

Although Henslow's way of displaying the plants is aesthetically pleasing, the beauty belies the impressive statistical approach to his work.

Henslow described this way of compiling his sheets (vouchers) as 'collation' to demonstrate the natural variation in plants. From this process he defined the characteristic of species. Most contemporaneous botanists such as W J Hooker from Glasgow then Kew, Charles Babbington his successor at Cambridge and JH Balfour from Edinburgh rarely placed more than one plant on the same herbarium sheet. Henslow's work culminated in publishing of his 'Catalogue of British plants, arranged according to the natural system' in 1829. From his knowledge as Professor of Mineralogy, Henslow applied Haüy's theory of crystals to produce a rigorous method of dividing plant species. Abbé Haüy used a mathematical formula to explain how complex crystals were transformations of a more basic crystals. Henslow was an aggregator or 'lumper' of plants (like basic crystals) whereas other botanists were 'splitters' dividing plants into species, he saw varieties of the same species.

He had an interest in hybridisation and proposed the identification of species, by trialling hybridisation. If the 'cross' or hybrid plant was fertile he proposed its parents were of the same species.

His paper 'On the examination of a hybrid digitalis' described in detail a hybrid foxglove and its parents which grew in Henslow's own garden, flowering between the 19th of June and 22nd July 1831.

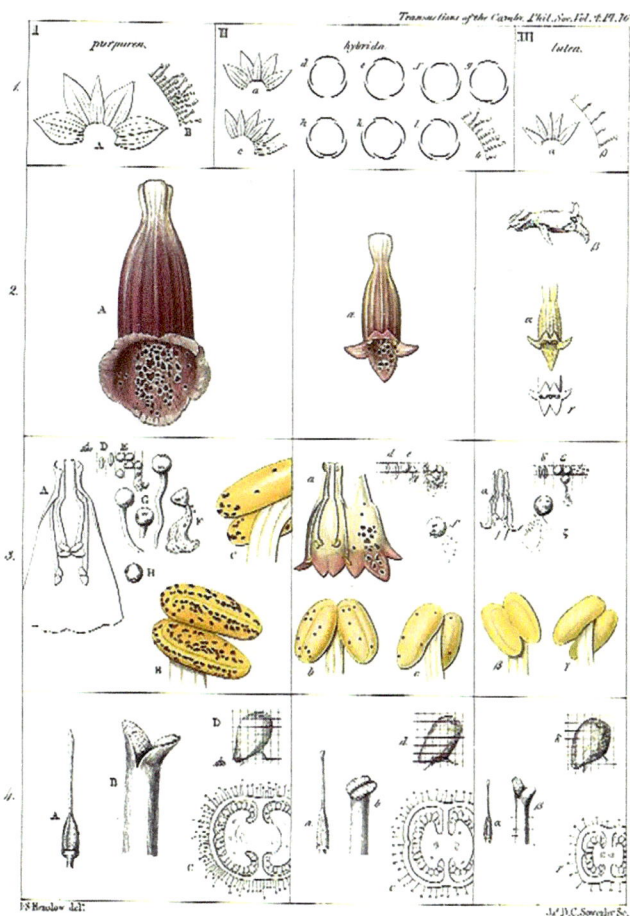

FIGURE 37
ILLUSTRATION FROM HENSLOW'S PAPER ON DIGITALIS

Henslow thoroughly explored the internal structure of the flower parts in both the parent plants and the hybrid. He concluded that although the parts appear the same, *'the functions of the reproductive apparatus appear to cease in the hybrid before they do in the parents'.*

His paper in 1832 on Paris quadrifolia (also known as herb Paris or true lovers knot) was the first plant population study published. Henslow used both his mathematical and botanical skills to assess 1500 specimens according to the number of leaves, sepals, petals, stamens in each sample. This is called meristic variation. The plants were gathered from Whitwell farm near Coton, Cambridgeshire by Henslow, his friends and students.

Henslow proposed that Paris was

'ever struggling to become double in all its parts'

FIGURE 38 PARIS QUADRIFOLIA SHOWING FOUR, FIVE AND SIX LEAVES
CAMBRIDGE UNIVERSITY HERBARIUM

Later when his famous Student Charles Darwin asked how isolated populations could show variation Henslow marked Darwin's correspondence with a single word.

"Paris".

On revising his "Catalogue' in 1835 he demoted 100 species to 'varieties', thereby challenging the great taxonomist botanists of the day such as Augustin De Candolle, William Hooker and John Lindley. Between 1821 to 1837 Henslow published 24 botanical papers. In the Spring of 1828, he became a founder contributor to John Claudius Loudon's Magazine of Natural History. Henslow's article was an account of the Cambridge Botanical Museum.

Henslow saw the need to have an arboretum, planting large trees in family groups. He identified variations in plants which might offer advantages over the parent plant. We are fortunate to witness some of his plantings from the nineteenth century at their ultimate size.

On the Main Avenue of the current Botanic Garden varieties of the Black Pines demonstrate this. The specimen from Austria, Pinus nigra ssp nigra with its downward sweeping branches with short stiff upright needles would survive better in snowy conditions. In contrast P. nigra ssp salzmannii from Mediterranean Spain (below right) has more upright branches bearing long flexuous needles.

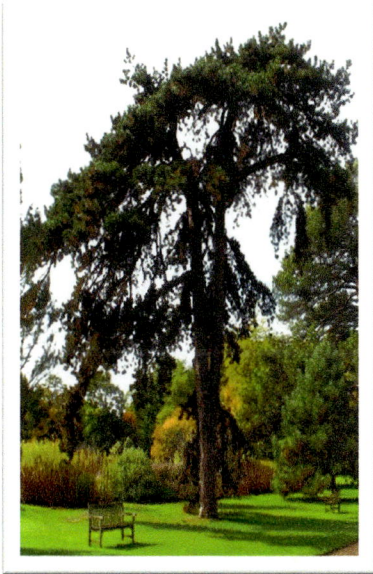

FIGURE 39
PINUS NIGRA SSP NIGRA

FIG 40
PINUS NIGRA SSP SALZMANNI
(PHOTO T HOOPER)

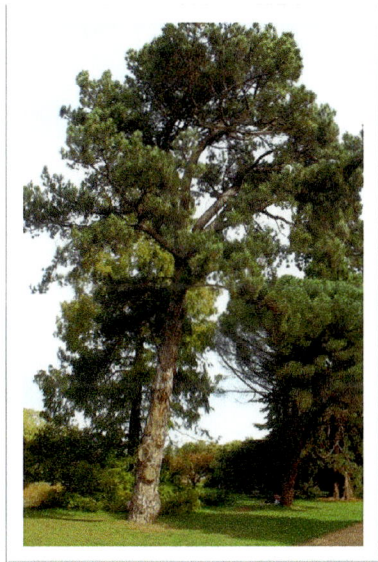

Changes in plants which occurred spontaneously in nature were referred to by both Henslow and Darwin as "monstrosities". These now referred to as mutations.

However, monster was a topical word in the early nineteenth century. Mary Shelley's 'Frankenstein' was published in 1818. The fictional Dr Victor Frankenstein's experiment to build a beautiful giant humanoid from various body parts resulted in a reviled 8-foot monster.

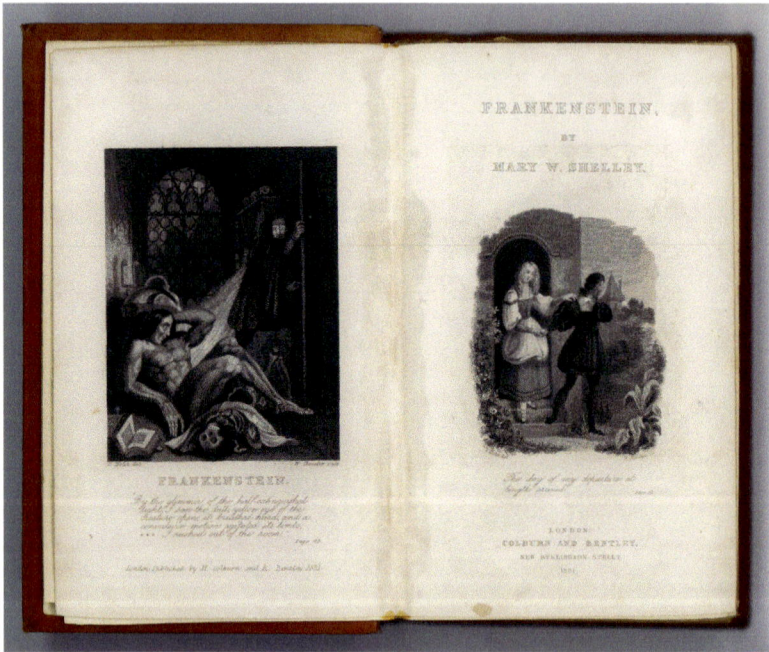

FIGURE 41
1832 COPY OF MARY SHELLEY'S FRANKENSTEIN.
ALAMY STOCK PHOTO

The book is thought of as one of the earliest science fiction novels and one can imagine it being a favourite with young students of the day.

Three beech trees were planted as observational trial namely the species tree Fagus sylvatica, F. sylvatica var heterophylla 'Asplenifolia', a cut-leaf variant and F. sylvatica 'Miltonensis' a weeping form of beech which is the result of grafting a garden mutant or monstrosity found in Milton Park, Northamptonshire in 1837.

FIGURE 42
FAGUS SYLVATICA CENTRE WITH 'VAR ASPLENIFOLIA'
ON LEFT AND 'MILTONENSIS' ON RIGHT, KATE HOOPER

FIGURE 43
LEAVES OF F. SYLVATICA AND F. SYLVATICA VAR ASPLENIFOLIA
PROFESSOR JOHN S PARKER

FIGURE 44
A. WHOLE TREE AND B. CLOSE
UP SHOWING GRAFTING FAGUS
SYLVATICA 'MILTONENSIS'
PHOTOS TIM HOOPER

The trees thrived, still give shade to the visitor and boast their differences to the East of Middle Walk in Cambridge Botanic Garden today.

Henslow was a great observer, and his genius was in noticing differences and variations. He would have passed these ideas on to Darwin urging him to look for differences. It is possible that Darwin would have reached his theory of evolution and natural selection, culminating in the publishing of 'On the Origin of the Species' if he had not studied with Henslow in Cambridge. However, without his mentor's influence and practical support, Darwin's career may have taken a very different course.

Robert Gunthe, founder of the Oxford History of Science Museum summed it up succinctly in 1921

'without Henslow there would have been no Darwin'.

Henslow's legacy is greater than just being Darwin's mentor. No one else was analysing plants with such mathematical rigour in the nineteenth century. He urged botanists to tabulate their results and not to ignore 'unsatisfactory results'. His Catalogue of the Plants of Britain utilised not only his botanical knowledge but his organisational skills to collate data from many sources to produce a unique and practical textbook. He was a good philosopher and scientist.

CHAPTER FIVE

Was Henslow a Social Reformer?

I started this project as I was perplexed as to why Henslow had left Cambridge in 1839 just as his dream of a large Botanic Garden was being realised. Looking at Henslow's time in Cambridge he did indeed have political ideals, took his university responsibilities seriously and was compelled to do what he considered to be the right thing. I will look at some of his roles in more detail, and in particular how he tried to mitigate discrimination and the class inequities of the time.

1836 saw Henslow and over 60 members of the Senate proposing the abolition of the religious tests which prevented Dissenters from taking degrees at Oxford and Cambridge. Dissenters was the term used to describe the diverse group of Protestants who did not align to the Church of England. One of Henslow's friends Richard Dawes, Fellow at Trinity College lost his expected appointment to Master of that college because of voting for the abolition of religious tests.

Dawes and Henslow continued to communicate when the former gave up his Fellowship and pursued his career in the Church. Dawes devoted his life to improving the education and wellbeing of the poor and became Dean of Hereford. The two continued to communicate by letter when Henslow became Rector of Hitcham.

Henslow was Chairman of a Cambridge Committee which successfully canvassed to re-elect Lord Palmerston as a University MP. Henslow had followed Palmerston from the Conservative Party to the Whigs in 1830. With John Lamb, Master of Corpus Christi, Henslow published a pamphlet to abolish the payment of expenses to 'out-voters' from the candidate they voted for. On 19th March 1835 bribery charges were aired at the Cambridge Lent Assizes. It was reported in the Cambridge Independent Press that Professor Henslow informed on Mr Fawcett, one of the accused. Henslow insisted that he was,

'acting under those principles he had always professed; felt it was his duty not to shirk'.

After this event Henslow was rewarded by the title of Common Informer, receiving abuse from his political opponents and graffiti like the image below which could be seen on the walls of Corpus Christi College into the 1960s.

FIGURE 45
LINO PRINT IMAGE OF 19TH CENTURY GRAFFITI, KATE HOOPER

A surprising role of 19th century Cambridge academics was that of Proctor, who patrolled the Cambridge streets. Henslow took his turn in 1830 from February to June. He made 22 arrests of 'wrongdoers' – women suspected of prostitution and leading the university gentleman astray.

In comparison with Adam Sedgwick, who was described as

'a tall black stalking figure scouring the high streets industriously seeking out sin',

Henslow was a lenient Proctor. Of his 22 arrests, 10 were released the next morning on the basis they would not sin again. In 1834 during his second period of office he arrested 10 women, releasing four including a certain Mary Ann Webb who had been arrested 24 times. Henslow released her as she was unwell and promised to go home. Henslow's sensitivity to the hardship of others is apparent.

Why did Henslow accept a parish living in 1837?

Between 1825 – 1835 Professor and Mrs Henslow had six children although one sadly died in infancy. Henslow supplemented his university fees which rose to £200 per annum for the Regius Chair of Botany, by teaching or 'cramming' poll men. These were the undergraduates who needed help to pass the Senate examination. The finances of the day equated to

'£300 a year as the boundary between keeping up a respectable middle-class appearance and a struggle,'

according to F Knight in his 1995 book on the Nineteenth Century Church and English Society. Henslow received £340 annually as Rector of Cholsey-cum-Moulsford in Berkshire (now in Oxfordshire) from 1832 to 1837. He had a reliable curate Richard Pinniger in residence, whom he joined during the college vacations, to tend to his Cholsey flock in person. Amongst the Cambridge and Oxford ordained it was common practice to appoint a curate to their parish, but continue to live in the university city, thereby allowing them to remain in active in academia.

In 1837 the Bishop of Ely on appointing Henslow as Rector of All Saints Church in Hitcham , Suffolk wrote that the Professor was,

'best calculated by his ability, activity and common sense to reform that populous, remote, and woefully neglected parish, where the duty of squire, magistrate and rector must all fall on the latter'

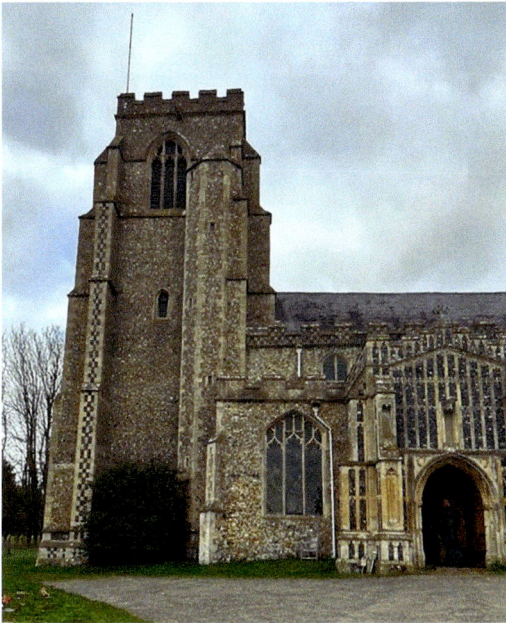

FIGURE 46
ALL SAINTS CHURCH,
HITCHAM
PHOTO KATE HOOPER

Henslow accepted the relatively lucrative 'living', it seemed the ideal solution for the Professor's financial worries, increasing his annual income to £1000 per year. Just 40 miles east of Cambridge, close to Stowmarket Station so Henslow hoped to continue teaching Botany to undergraduates, oversee the New Botanic Garden and attend to his congregations.

However, Henslow found the parish of Hitcham in a very dire situation. John Staverton Matthew the incumbent for the previous 36 years was described as easy going and of having no desire to improve his parishioners' 'temporal or spiritual wellbeing'. His Sunday congregations were in single figures. Parishioners were living in poverty, with half the population receiving subsistence level benefits from the village charity. The workers were dependent on seasonal farm employment but with little support from the landowners. High illiteracy rates and unemployment led to poor housing, lack of food and clothing. Many residents turned to crime. The convicted criminal rate in Hitcham in 1839 was one in 365 people. The task was challenging even for his reliable curate from Cholsey, Richard Pinniger, who left after two years.

That year, 1839, Henslow moved permanently to Hitcham, returning to teach his University Botany Course for 3 months in the Summer Term.

FIGURE 47
LINO PRINT OF HITCHAM RECTORY, JACK FAWDRY TATHAM

Social unrest amongst unemployed labourers peaked in the 1840s. There were 83 committals for arson from 1843 to 1847.

By 1841 Henslow had facilitated a coal club, children's clothing club, medical club, benefits club and wives club. Initially farmers agreed to transport the coal for free (provided someone else paid for the coal) but an allotment scheme was strongly opposed. Henslow received this angry letter from a farmer,

" I am sorry to say it appears you are one of those philanthropic gentlemen who wish to make themselves popular with the lower classes of society at the expense of the farmer,........I will never cart another ton of coal for the poor so long as this sub-letting system is in existence."

Henslow responded by digging up the Rectory garden to provide a small number of plots, allowing his hungry parishioners to grow some food for their families. He introduced an Annual Horticultural Show, providing cups for produce and ploughing competitions.

For Henslow there was added pressure of being both magistrate and parson. Three of his parishioners were prosecuted for sheep-stealing in 1842. They appeared before the Bury Magistrates who included Robert Mabeltoft, the owner of Hitcham Hall. A fourth man turned Queen's evidence, thereby gaining his freedom and his witness statement survives,

'I went to Mr Hatton's barn-yard with the three prisoners; we took two sheep away from the yard to the second field from the barn; we killed the animals there, skinned them, ... and carried the mutton home to my house, where we each had a quarter of the sheep.'

The three convicted men were sentenced to transportation to Australia for 15 years. Three days later Henslow preached a sermon condemning the crimes, but mindful of those present.

'I have no desire to dwell upon the particular circumstances which have led to these wretched results. It would be too painful to some of you,'

It was unlikely the men would ever return to Hitcham, and their wives and families were left to fend for themselves. There were 83 committals for arson from 1843 to 1847. Henslow wrote to William Whewell, (Master of Trinity College and his successor as Professor of Mineralogy) on 1st March 1844,

'We have almost nightly fires about the neighbourhood and as I was lecturing at Hadleigh on Wednesday, a cry of fire interrupted...'

George Henslow his son described how the Henslow family extracted starch from rotten potatoes in 1845 by grating and sieving the potato into cold water. The resultant brown starch was rinsed 2-3 times before it was white. This was dried in the sun or a warm room in muslin bags which had to be kneaded to prevent clotting. The white potato flour could then be used in baking. Their method was circulated around Hitcham and presented to the Hadleigh Farmers Club on Friday 13th September 1845. Henslow wished to help the villagers use the substandard potato as safe food . The potato famine was affecting the poor on both sides of the Irish Sea.

Henslow utilised his love of science and lifelong education to help the farming community and increase food production, thereby helping to reduce food poverty. George Henslow wrote about a family holiday to Felixstowe when his father noted the presence of coprolites (fossilised dung) in the cliffs in a deposit called Red Crag. Henslow Senior postulated this would make this a good plant fertiliser. Having conducted trials to prove this, he discussed his findings with local farmers. Henslow's idea was taken up by Edward Packard in Ipswich (hence the poetically named Coprolite Street in Ipswich.) His son Edward Packard, Junior bought out another fertiliser company from Thetford in 1919, forming 'Packard and James Fisons'. The company name simplified to 'Fisons Ltd' in 1942, becoming internationally renowned for changing agriculture across the globe. Henslow wrote about wheat midge, ergot on corn and the vitality of seed amongst other topics in his Letters to the Farmers of Suffolk.

His family and friends helped fund trips to Ipswich and London for groups of Hitcham residents. The London expedition for twenty people over 3 days, included visits to the Great Exhibition, The Polytechnic, The Zoological Gardens and Kew Gardens.

However, his social conscience and ambition is probably best demonstrated by his successful trip to Cambridge with over 200 Hitcham villagers in 1854. A beautifully illustrated pocket-sized pamphlet was produced for the day with the itinerary, with drawings of notable buildings such at Kings College Chapel, St John's and the Round Church. There were also illustrations of plants from the Botanic Garden. Henslow was keen to share the tropical plants with his Suffolk villagers. This gift of experiencing plants from different climates is still available to every visitor to the Cambridge Botanic Garden.

FIGURE 48
DETAIL FROM HITCHAM TO CAMBRIDGE EXCURSION PAMPHLET 1854
HITCHAM VESTRY

The villagers had to get themselves to and home from Stowmarket Railway Station, roughly sixteen miles in total. Once in Cambridge they received a guided tour from Henslow himself and were treated to dinner and tea at Downing College, even some farmers attended.

Jenyns writes

"To give some idea of the pains taken and the costs incurred , by Professor Henslow to instruct and amuse the whole party, ... distributed among them for the occasion :-

250 of the above programmes
36 maps of Cambridge
50 sets of plates of the twelve colleges
More than 100 single prints of ditto
200 plates of some of the more remarkable plants in the Botanic Garden

One labourer commented to the Professor Henslow after seeing objects in a museum,

"Our heads would not be so full of drink if we had such things to occupy our minds"

With such an affirmation, along with the silver cup presented to him by the farmers Henslow must have been fired up for continuing his project of education for social reform.

He continued to support and develop the Ipswich Museum. He brought small artefacts to the Hitcham Village Shows such as pearls from British molluscs, ostrich eggs and tobacco plants. He traced out the dimensions of the giant redwood (Sequoiadendron gigantea) on Hitcham Rectory lawn. He lectured to evening groups such as the Hadleigh Farmers and Royston Mechanics. In February 1859 Henslow recorded the success of classes for adults; his daughter teaching young women every Monday afternoon and his curate the young men on Tuesday and Thursday evenings.

However, Henslow reminded parents that children found it easier to

'master the rudiments of learning when young'.

FIGURE 49
TOWN COTTAGE , PREVIOUSLY HITCHAM SCHOOL, KATE HOOPER

When Henslow took on the Parish of Hitcham in 1837, there was no village school and the absent landowner had no interest in providing one. As the Bishop had commented, the responsibilities fell on the Rector. Henslow and his family had to bear the cost of acquiring and running the school. Initially Henslow taught botany every Monday afternoon. Although aimed at children under 14 years the syllabus was barely simplified from what Henslow taught his undergraduates.

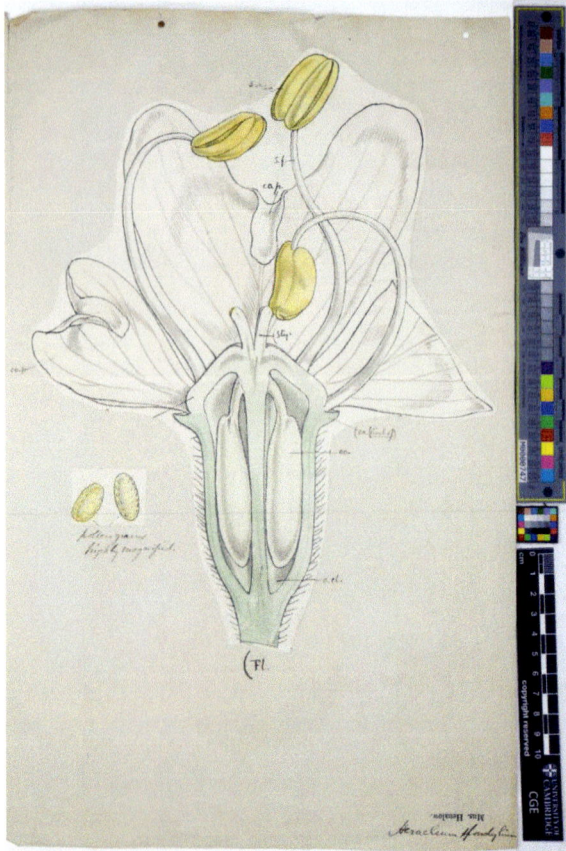

FIGURE 50 TYPICAL HENSLOW TEACHING ILLUSTRATION,
CAMBRIDGE UNIVERSITY HERBARIUM

Prizes were awarded to those children achieving the highest
marks in the class tests, their homework and for the species
they identified in flower in the summer. Botanical Excursions
could only be attended by those achieving high enough marks at
the Monday Lessons. The wildflower meadows are still enjoyed
today in Hitcham.

FIGURE 51
HITCHAM WILDFLOWER MEADOW WITH ARRAN.
PHOTOGRAPH, DR JANE FAIRWEATHER

An excerpt from the School botany pamphlet follows

VILLAGE-SCHOOL BOTANY

Children wishing to learn Botany will be placed in the 3rd Class when they have learnt to spell the following words

Class	Division	Section
(I. Exercise)	(II. Ex)	(IV Ex.)

	1..Angiospermous	1.Thalamifloral
1. Dicotyledons		2. Calycifloral
		3. Corollifloral
		(V. Ex)
	2. Gymnospermous	4. Incomplete
	(III.Ex)	
2. Monocotyledons	1. Petaloid 1. Superior	
	2. Inferior	
	2. Glumaceous	
3. Acotyledons		

==

Children in the 3rd Class who have learnt how to fill in the first column of the Floral Schedule, and to spell correctly the following words , will be raised to the Second Class.

Pistils &
Carpels   of Ovary (with Ovules), Style , and Stigma.

Stamens, of Filament and Anther (with Pollen).

Corolla, of Petals
Calyx, of Sepals.   Or Perianth, of Leaves.

==

Children in the 2nd Class who have learnt how to fill in the second column of the Floral schedule, and to spell correctly the following words will be raised to the 1st Class.........

FIGURE 52
REPRODUCTION OF EXCERPT FROM HITCHAM SCHOOL BOTANY PAMPHLET,
KATE HOOPER

80

FIGURE 53

ANGELICA SYLVESTRIS, CAMBRIDGE UNIVERSITY HERBARIUM

The herbarium sheet shows Angelica sylvestris, collected for Henslow by A. Carpenter, from Portishead, Bristol in 1839. We know that the Hitcham school children looked at angelica as they were rewarded by sweetmeats made from the plants they were studying. Henslow wrote to George Knights (his friend and the Curator of Ipswich Museum) on 7th September 1855,

'I have promised my botanical schoolchildren some angelica as a botanical sweetmeat; would you be so kind as to procure me about 2/6d worth and either send it to me or bring it to me on the 19th'

FIGURE 54
CANDIED ANGELICA, TIM HOOPER

The children were taught how to prepare herbarium specimens or vouchers. Drying, then pressing the plant material, before mounting it on paper and labelling it correctly. Some of his students went on to teach.

Notably Harriet Sewell (1842- 1936) was the first pupil-teacher. She was awarded first prize for identifying more than 159 species of plants in 1858. Harriet received a Queen's scholarship for teacher training college aged twenty. She later became a governess and travelled widely with her employers, continuing to collect and record the plants she found. Her family in Hitcham were very proud of Aunt Harriet's scrapbook. It was clear that Henslow valued the education of women in his support of his talented pupils.

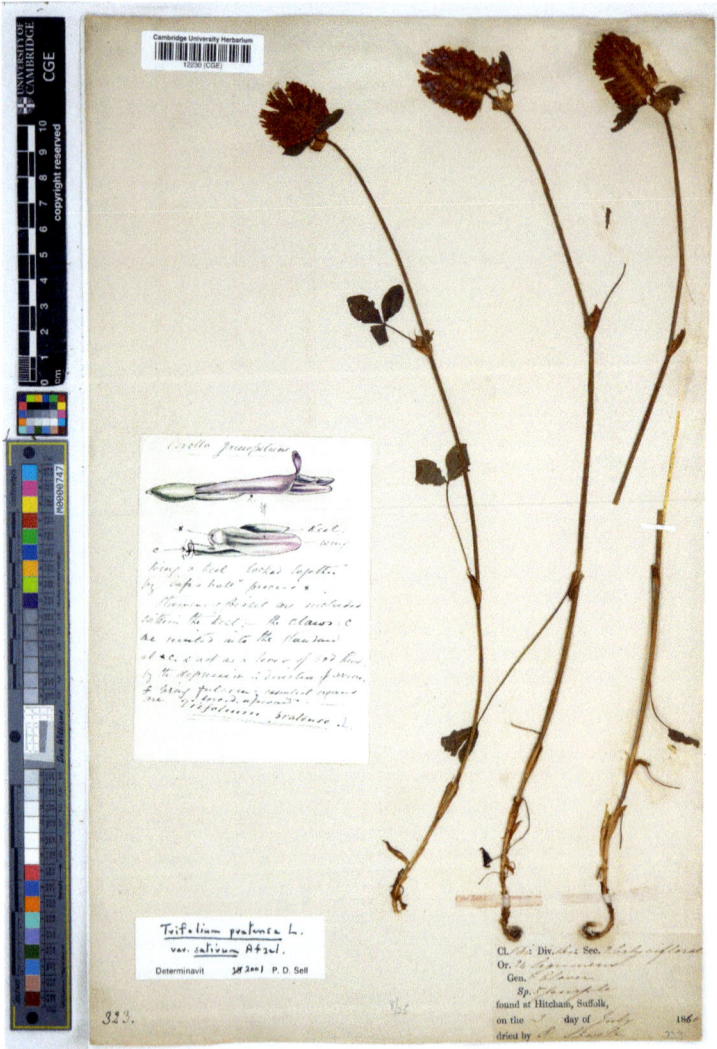

FIGURE 55
TRIFOLIUM PRATENSE, COLLECTED BY HARRIET SEWELL, WITH HAND
DRAWN ILLUSTRATION, CAMBRIDGE UNIVERSITY HERBARIUM

FIGURE 56
PRIMULA VERIS COLLECTED BY HARRIET SEWELL WITH TEXTBOOK
ILLUSTRATIONS TYPICAL OF HENSLOW, CAMBRIDGE UNIVERSITY HERBARIUM

Charles Darwin wrote to Henslow in 1855 asking him to send seeds collected by 'his little girls' so he could carry our plant experiments to aid his research. Harriet Sewell was almost certainly one of these little girls. Darwin requested 22 different species, and he offered to pay the pupils 3d per packet (this would equate to approximately £3 today)

"it will put a few shillings in their pockets and would be an ENORMOUS advantage to me, for I grudge the time to collect the seeds, more especially, as I have to learn the plants!"

It appeared that with Henslow's tuition those little girls' botanical knowledge surpassed that of Charles Darwin.

John Stevens Henslow dedicated his life to the service of others. In standing up to corruption, he risked his career in Cambridge. He then gave up his City life to be with his parish. As a Rector he took his responsibility to his flock beyond their spiritual and educational needs. He provided practical help for those on the poverty line. He campaigned at a national level, presenting his paper on the state of the 'Labouring Population' to Parliament.

I think Henslow has earned the title of social reformer.

CHAPTER SIX

Was Henslow a Good Friend?

Henslow was a happy person and as Leonard Jenyns wrote

'his desire and endeavour was to make others as happy as himself'

He struck up a lasting friendship with Leonard Jenyns in 1820 when the latter was an undergraduate at Cambridge. They enjoyed nature trails together in Bedfordshire and South Cambridgeshire. Henslow visited Jenyns family home at Bottisham and three years later married Leonard's sister Harriet. Leonard's affection and admiration is apparent in his 'Memoir of the Rev John Steven Henslow' written in 1862. Jenyns notes how Henslow was always ready 'to encourage, to advise and to assist' him and particularly credits his brother-inlaw's generosity when he published 'Monograph on the British Species of Cyclas and Pisidium'. Jenyns was another clergyman naturalist first as Curate in Swaffham Bulbeck, then acquiring his own living near Bath.

On a geological field trip to the Isle of Wight in the Spring of 1819, Henslow not only discovered an ammonite but a friend with mutual interests. Cambridge graduate Adam Sedgwick had decided to pursue a college fellowship, funding himself with private tutoring. His financial independence on achieving fellowship at Trinity College in 1810 enabled him to travel around Europe. He was so inspired by the scenery in Switzerland, he sought to spend more time outdoors. He realised that his desire to understand the Natural World required study of other subjects rather than just mathematics. The ideal opportunity arose when the Woodwardian Chair of Geology became available in 1818. Sedgwick threw himself into the role, particularly enjoying field trips to various mines around the United Kingdom. Henslow accompanied him on many of these trips. The pair of them hatched the plan to form the Cambridge Philosophical Society as previously discussed.

Henslow was very close to fellow undergraduate Marmaduke Ramsay who pipped him to 15th place in their final exams. Ramsay who became a Fellow and Tutor of Jesus College, died in 1831 affecting Henslow significantly. Charles Darwin had invited Henslow and Ramsay to join him on an expedition to the Canary islands that year. Henslow wrote on 24th August informing Darwin of Ramsay's death and therefore his reason for not travelling to Tenerife. The tragic loss of a close friend changed not only Henslow's life, but that of Charles Darwin. In the same August letter, Henslow informed Darwin that he had put Charles' name forward as Gentleman Companion to Captain FitzRoy who was commencing a geographical survey on HMS Beagle.

Charles Robert Darwin was born on the same day as Abraham Lincoln, 12th February 1809. With three older sisters and his brother Erasmus, Charles was the fifth child of Dr Robert Darwin, a successful surgeon and Susannah (née Wedgwood). His grandfather Erasmus Darwin (after whom his older brother was named) was a physician with an interest in engineering and botany. Erasmus challenged the contemporary British botanists with his racy poem 'The Loves of the Plants'. The establishment were censoring the work of Swedish botanist Linnaeus by removing any mention of male and female flower parts. Erasmus wrote Zoönomia in 1794 which proposed that God had caused the world but after that left Creation to run and improve itself. The Darwins were not averse to causing controversy when challenging human dogma. Charles went to Cambridge aged 19, with a view to joining the clergy, having found medicine at Edinburgh was not to his liking.

Charles was a reluctant student but was inspired by John Stevens Henslow, attending his Botany course three times. Darwin had read, avidly, 'Natural Theology, or Evidences of the Existence and Attributes of the Deity' written in 1802 by William Paley, who was a liberal, anti-slavery, moral philosopher. Paley postulated in his 'watchmaker' argument that living beings are more complex than anything designed by human hands Although Paley's arguments are dismissed by many today and Darwin is charged with 'killing off Paley', Darwin left Cambridge a 'Paleyite'. This was not only because of his books, which were standard 19th Century Cambridge theology teaching, but because of Henslow's example. The way Henslow treated Darwin 'was genuinely good, patient, selfless and kind' as E L Peterson, Darwin biographer writes.

Charles Darwin became known as "the Man who walked with Henslow"

FIGURE 57
DARWIN AND HENSLOW ON A CAMBRIDGESHIRE FIELD TRIP.
JACK FAWDRY TATHAM

Following a field trip with Henslow and the rest of the class to the ericaceous bog area of Gamlingay, Cambridgeshire, fellow student John Rodwell wrote *'We once had a trip to Gamlingay Heath in search of Natter-jacks. Darwin was very successful in detecting the haunts of these pretty reptiles and catching them. He brought several to Henslow who said laughingly – 'Well Darwin, are you going to make Natter-jack pie?'*

90

FIGURE 58
LINO PRINT BY J FAWDRY TATHAM

Maybe it was this performance that led Henslow to recommend Charles Darwin as gentleman companion to Captain Fitzroy and naturalist on the Beagle voyage, writing to him that he was the

'best qualified person I know of - not on the supposition of yr. being a finished naturalist, but as amply collecting, observing & noting anything new to be noted'.

FIGURE 59 THE BEAGLE,
ALAMY STOCK PHOTO

Henslow provided him with a rain gauge and an iron net for shells for his voyage. Darwin made the necessary contacts to join the voyage despite the numerous objections from his own father. Darwin wrote to Henslow,

'Even if I was to go my Father disliking would take away all energy, & I should want a good stock of that – Again I must thank you: it adds a little to the heavy but pleasant load of gratitude which I owe to you. –"

Fortunately, Charles had a powerful ally, his uncle Josiah Wedgwood who suggested to his brother-in-law, Dr Robert Darwin, that Charles might not spend the next few years wisely if was not allowed to go. The Beagle with Darwin on board set sail on 27th December 1831.

Communication between Henslow and Darwin was hampered by the distances involved. In Valparaiso on 24th July 1834 Darwin received two letters from Henslow, dated January 15th, 1833, and 12th December 1833. He wrote back immediately acknowledging how happy he was to receive them but regretting the delay as he felt his collections had been poor.

Henslow had written in the January letter,

'So far from being disappointed with the Box – I think you have done wonders – as I know you do not confine yourself to collecting but are careful to describe. Most of the plants are desirable to me. Avoid sending scraps. Make the specimens as perfect as you can, root, flowers & leaves and you can't go wrong'.

FIGURE 60
VULPIA TENELLA COLLECTED BY DARWIN IN PATAGONIA
CAMBRIDGE UNIVERSITY HERBARIUM

Henslow received all the Beagle specimens and distributed them to interested parties. He was gifted with the 2,600 "plants for Henslow". Hence, they are mounted on Henslow's own printed Herbarium paper and are preserved today in the Cambridge University Herbarium. The identification was completed by Joseph Hooker ten years later. In a typically generous gesture, the letters from Darwin in South America were edited by Henslow and published at his own expense, so Darwin returned a famous traveller and natural historian.

In his 1837 paper on Opuntia (prickly pear) Henslow describes Opuntia darwinii (which he has named after his 'friend' C Darwin Esq.) and Opuntia galapageia, for which he also claims to be indebted to Mr Darwin for, as the specimen was from James's Island in the Galapagos. O. darwinii was collected at Port Desire 47 degrees south in Patagonia. Darwin saw similar plants at 49 degrees, which Henslow notes as the most southerly recorded for that species. We are fortunate in Cambridge University Herbarium, to have the specimens that Darwin collected.

FIGURE 61
OPUNTIA GALAPAGEIA COLLECTED BY DARWIN FROM JAMES'S ISLAND, 1835
CAMBRIDGE UNIVERSITY HERBARIUM

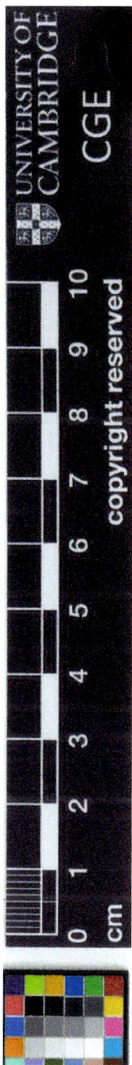

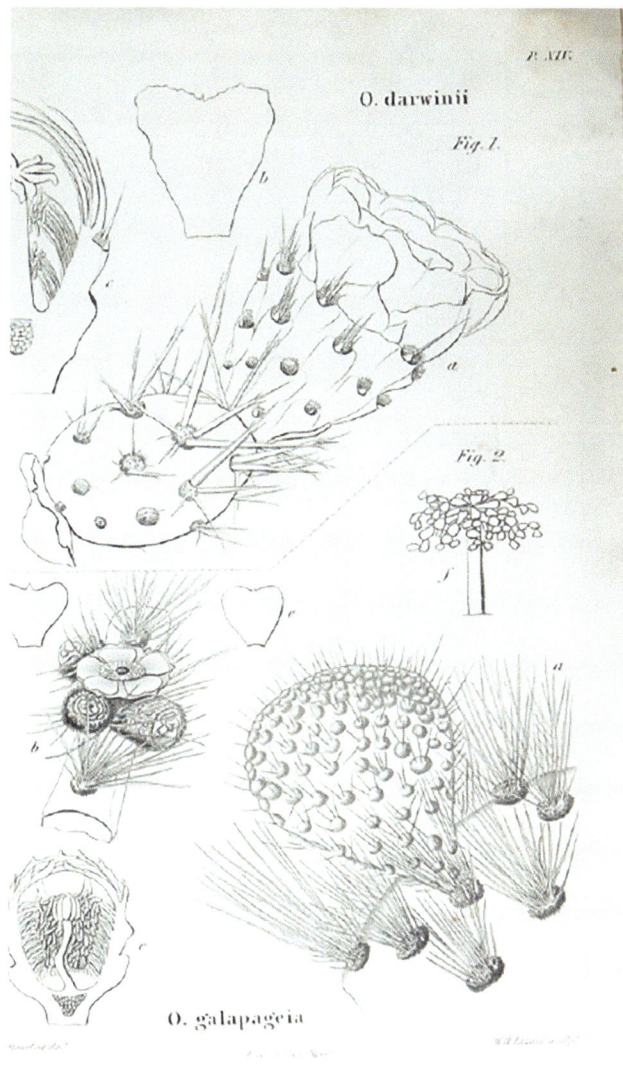

FIGURE 62
ILLUSTRATION PLATE DRAWN BY HENSLOW SHOWING TWO SPECIES OF
OPUNTIA, CAMBRIDGE UNIVERSITY HERBARIUM

Darwin pondered on his findings and researched the current knowledge extensively on his return in 1836. His 'wakeup call' arrived in 1858. Albert Russel Wallace a young naturalist sent Darwin a draft paper 'On the Tendency of varieties to depart indefinitely from the Original Type'. Darwin decided to publish his 'sketch' on the same day as Wallace's paper, both were read out at the Linnean Society on 1st July 1858. Darwin had hoped his work would be discovered posthumously but was now concerned his years of work would be discounted if Wallace's theory was published first. These papers did not shock the scientific world , Darwin decided to find a publisher.

'On the Origin of the Species by Natural Selection' was released 24th November 1859. The first 1,250 copies sold quickly to both scientists and lay readers. Six further editions were released during Darwin's lifetime and after hearing that a group of Lancashire labourers had clubbed together to buy a copy, Darwin instructed his publisher to make it more affordable. However, his standing in academia had plummeted.

Henslow in his own words 'stuck up for' Darwin when his Cambridge friends Sedgwick and William Clark (Professor of Anatomy) vehemently denounced Darwin's theories at the Cambridge Philosophical Society on May 7th, 1860.

Henslow wrote to his son-in-law Joseph Hooker, that he was,

'- refusing to allow that he (Darwin) was guided by any but truthful motives and declaring that he believed he was exalting & not debasing our views of a Creator.'

Professor Henslow chaired the Oxford meeting of The British Association in June 1860, although his own health was failing. He stepped in when the person due to chair failed to turn up, perhaps the latter had known it would be a difficult meeting to control. Four attendees had to be silenced. Charles Darwin was too ill to attend. The tempers were raging between Bishop Sam Wilberforce and Thomas Huxley who clashed over the proposed theory of man's evolution from animals. Henslow apparently employed great tact and control over the opposing factions.

FIGURE 63
LINO PRINT OF DARWIN,
A CHIMP AND BIRDS.
JACK FAWDRY TATHAM

It appeared Henslow thought Darwin had published his theory too soon without enough scientific back up. Darwin was disappointed his mentor and hero did not write to him directly about the subject. Henslow visited Darwin for three days in February 1860 and we can imagine the pair discussed the subject at length. Charles Darwin wrote on 15th February to his friend Charles Lyell during Henslow's stay,

'he [Henslow] says though he cannot go as far as I do, he can give no good reason why he should not'

Charles Darwin was keen to impress his mentor who had introduced him to so many ideas from the interesting guests at the Cambridge evening gatherings at John and Harriet's home.

One such guests at a Henslows' soiree, was the American French artist John James Audubon who visited Cambridge to promote his bird and flower engravings Henslow described Audubon as *very amiable, very zealous, and deserves to be extensively patronised.'*

Henslow's generous support naming a sparrow after him, Ammodramus henslowii

FIGURE 64
HENSLOW'S SPARROW, LINO
PRINT BY KATE HOOPER

We can imagine Henslow would have been proud of his unconventional student when in 1862 Darwin published his first book purely on plants 'Fertilisation of Orchids', sadly Henslow had died in 1861. Darwin's book was received with widespread critical acclaim. The American Botanist, Asa Gray reviewing the book in Silliman's Journal of Science wrote of the *'fascination it must have for even slightly instructed readers.'* Darwin's self-esteem was restored – *'Now I can confidently defy the world.'* Ten years later Darwin wrote in his autobiography that Henslow

'influenced my whole career more than any other'.

In summary Henslow was a good friend to many, too numerous to mention in this small book - but he was one of Darwin's best friends.

CHAPTER SEVEN

Was Henslow a good family man?

Leonard Jenyns observed 'the loyal and apparently equitable marriage' of his sister Harriet and John Stevens Henslow when describing his brother-in-law's opportunity to sail on the Beagle in 1831. (Jenyns was also offered the post of gentleman's companion to Captain Fitzroy.)

'Henslow himself was not very far from accepting it for Mrs Henslow most generously and without being asked gave her consent, but she looked so miserable that Henslow at once settled the point.'

It was apparent Mr and Mrs Henslow felt very responsible for the education of their children, especially their daughters as they remained at home, whereas their sons went to boarding school. Harriet was an accomplished writer and knowledgeable about the arts, music and literature.

Henslow encouraged their children to study botany, and he used his their daughters' illustrations in his educational material. Their eldest daughter was the successful school mistress of Hitcham School for some time.

George Henslow described with warmth, the collection of wasp nests, toads, slow-worms, harvest mice and butterflies in their home. In 'On the Origin of the Species' Darwin described how Professor Henslow's harvest mice used their tails to climb branches in their cage.

FIGURE 65
HARVEST MICE USING THEIR TAILS TO CLIMB (ALAMY)

George Henslow enjoyed sharing the story of his father in Hitcham Rectory Garden, stopping, whilst in mid conversation with a visiting Judge, to run in for his butterfly net to catch the rare Camberwell Beauty.

FIGURE 66
CAMBERWELL BEAUTY, JACK FAWDRY TATHAM

FIGURE 67 ANAGELLIS MONELLI HERBARIUM SHEET
CAMBRIDGE UNIVERSITY HERBARIUM

This herbarium sheet demonstrates the correspondence between John and his lawyer brother Henry, regarding the propagation of Anagallis seed. In his St. Albans' garden in Hertfordshire, Henry raised a pink-flowered plant from the seed that John had collected from a blue-flowered plant. The pink petals are still visible on the herbarium sheet dated 1838.

106

John Stevens Henslow Family Tree

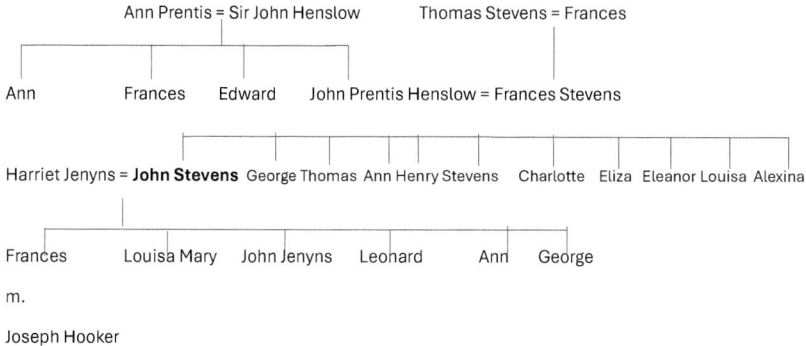

Ann Prentis = Sir John Henslow   Thomas Stevens = Frances

Ann   Frances   Edward   John Prentis Henslow = Frances Stevens

Harriet Jenyns = **John Stevens** George Thomas Ann Henry Stevens   Charlotte Eliza Eleanor Louisa Alexina

Frances   Louisa Mary   John Jenyns   Leonard   Ann   George
m.

Joseph Hooker

FIGURE 68
FAMILY TREE OF JOHN STEVENS HENSLOW, TIM HOOPER

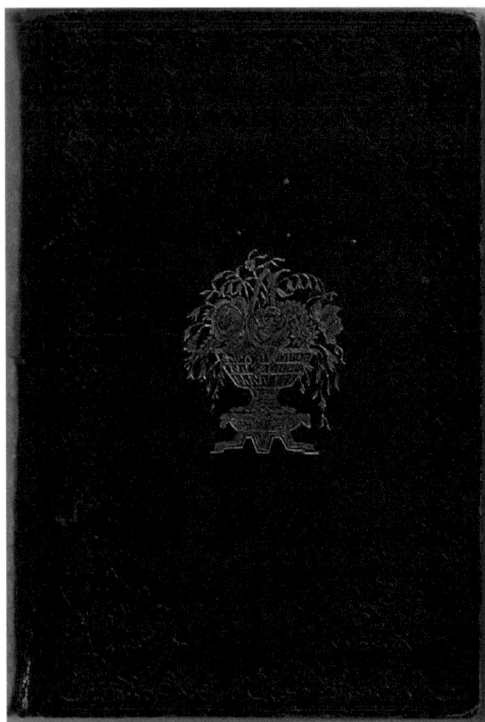

FIGURE 69
COVER OF BOUQUET DE SOUVENIRS, KATE HOOPER

Le Bouquet of Souvenirs, published in 1840 was written by Henslow, with two friends. His dedication reads

My Dear Sister,

In complying with your request that I furnish you with a popular description of the several plants featured in
'A Wreath of Friendship,'

I must risk my reputation as a Botanist and hazard my character, by being thought pedantic, by those unaccustomed to the use of technical terms.

Yours affectionately,
J.S. HENSLOW, Cambridge.

This volume illustrated with 25 colour plates of plants ranging from moss to roses, is accompanied by poems and seasonal observations. Henslow is credited with the botanical portion and there is a useful glossary of botanical terms at the back. There is a quote from a play called The Manor House which describes weaving garlands with friends as 'wreaths of friendships'.

Henslow's love for his sister appears to have surpassed his concern for any damage to his reputation, that association with this sentimental book might bring.

John Stevens Henslow made sure his relatives were looked after. Harriet and John moved in with Frances, his mother, during her final illness. She was laid to rest in Hitcham Graveyard in 1856. Henslow's maiden aunts Ann and Frances supplied plants for him whilst on holiday in Devon in 1826, as shown on the detail from the following herbarium sheet.

Ann Henslow was buried near her sister -in- law, Frances, in Hitcham in 1857, suggesting she too was nursed in Suffolk.

FIGURE 70
HARTS TONGUE FERN COLLATION, CAMBRIDGE UNIVERSITY HERBARIUM.

Parish records show Henslow's grandchildren William, Harriet Ann and Anna were all born in Hitcham, which may show how much his children valued their family home.

Dr Joseph Hooker, son of William Jackson Hooker, became close friends with Henslow after marrying the latter's eldest daughter Frances. Joseph, who was medically qualified as well as being a geographical botanist and skilled taxonomist, sat with Henslow during his final days and described his death as having left *'a blank in my existence never to be replaced. Quite apart from considerations matrimonial Henslow has had more influence over my life and conduct than any other man, so good, so calm, so wise .... He was one of those friends found late in life to be a lamp unto our path.'*

110

John Stevens Henslow was loved by his family and I think this is evidenced not only by the memoirs, but the collections and botanical art which survived him. Far from alienating them with his passions , his extended family supported him in collecting and sharing his discoveries of the Natural World.

John Stevens Henslow was an inspirational family man.

FIGURE 71
HENSLOW IN LATER LIFE, ALAMY STOCK PHOTO

EPILOGUE

John Stevens Henslow died at home on May 16th, 1861. Harriet had died almost four years earlier. He had instructed how the best parts of his collections were to be divided between the museums of Cambridge, Ipswich and Kew.

Henslow requested a simple funeral therefore only his immediate family accompanied his coffin from the Rectory. Nonetheless they were soon joined by many villagers, the Mayor of Ipswich, other custodians of the Ipswich Museum and a large delegation of the clergy. Jenyns wrote that the church and churchyard were full of parishioners. His brother-in-law also stated the grief shown that day in Hitcham, was matched by the University and the scientific world.

I agree with Professor Beverley Glover, current Director of Cambridge University Botanic Garden that John Stevens Henslow was a polymath. This quality was celebrated by the Victorians whereas subsequent generations have esteemed those with narrower focus. Henslow has been described as

'the man who knew everything'.

He, being a modest man, would disagree with this. However, his keen enquiring active brain has contributed so much to the world, not only to Cambridge, Hitcham and Ipswich.

Now if anyone asks you

"Who was Henslow?"

I hope you can give them
a full reply.

CHRONOLOGY

1796 Born in Frindsbury near Rochester Kent

1804 Enrolled to Mr & Mrs Dillon's private school in Rochester

Then later that year to The Rochester Free School

1805 Pupil at Rev William Jephson's boarding school in Camberwell

1811 Received Levaillant's "Travels in Africa" as a school prize

1814 Entered St John's College Cambridge

1815 Invented a double layered net to collect small crustaceans

1817 Polybius henslowii named after him by Dr William Leach of British Museum after Henslow discovered this new species of crab in North Devon.

1818 Completed BA in Mathematics Tripos

1818 Adam Sedgwick appointed to Woodwardian Professor of Geology and Henslow begins to attend his lectures. Elected as Fellow of Linnaean Society

1819 Field trip to Isle of Wight with Sedgwick

> Led Geology field trip to Isle of Man for students
>
> Elected Fellow of the Geological Society.
>
> With Sedgwick and Clarke arranged the first meeting of the Cambridge Philosophical Society

1820 Met Leonard Jenyns

1821 Geology expedition to Anglesey for students

1821 Cambridge Philosophical Society established

1822 Dr E.D. Clarke, Professor of Mineralogy died

1823 Professor of Mineralogy Henslow published his new syllabus in mineralogy

1823 Married Harriet Jenyns

1824 Ordained deacon in April and as priest in November, in common with half of his contemporary Cambridge graduates

1825 Rev Thomas Martyn, Professor of Botany died. Henslow was appointed to Chair of Botany

1831 The University of Cambridge bought 40 acres of farmland from Trinity Hall for the New Botanic Gardens after persuasion from Henslow

> Marmaduke Ramsay died

> Brother George died

> Henslow recommended Darwin to Fitzroy as a companion on The Beagle

1833 Vicar of Cholsey-cum-Moulsford in Berkshire. He employed a curate and spent the long vacations there

1833 Campaigned for political electoral reform to end bribery, leading to the graffti in Corpus Christi college, 'Henslow Common Informer'

1836 Darwin returned from the Beagle Expedition and sends his samples to Henslow

1836 Henslow published 'Principles of Physiological and Descriptive Botany

1837 Presented with the living of Hitcham, Suffolk

1839 Moved permanently to Hitcham

1842 Spoke at Hadleigh Farmers Club about low wages and crop rotation

1843 Discovered coprolites in Felixstowe

1843/4 Archaeological dig of Roman burial mounds, Eastlow Hill, Rougham, Suffolk

1844 Following unrest in farm worker communities published 'Enquiry into present condition of labouring population in Suffolk'

1846 Cambridge Botanic Garden opened on its Bateman Street site

1847 One of the founders of Ipswich Museum

1848 Founding Vice-President of the Bury St Edmunds and West Suffolk Archaeological Institute

Hitcham village excursions by train commenced

1849 Hitcham Allotments established

1850 Supplies William Hooker with specimens for Kew Garden Museum

First Hitcham Horticultural Show

Adult Literacy Classes commenced in Hitcham Welcomed Prince Albert on a visit to Ipswich Museum.

1851 Daughter Frances married Joseph Hooker

1857 Harriet Henslow, his wife died

1859 Charles Darwin published On the Origin of the Species 1860 Henslow Chairman Natural History Debate in Oxford.

Botany Classes delivered to the Royal family at Buckingham Palace

1861 February Lecture at Ipswich Museum

March Prepared the Honours Papers for Natural Science Tripos, Cambridge

May 16th died in Hitcham

LIST OF ILLUSTRATIONS

CHAPTER ONE

Fig 1 Lino print of Henslow as a young man by Jack Fawdry Tatham

Fig 2 Lino print of Henslow as a child carrying a giant puffball by Jack Fawdry Tatham

Fig 3 Aerial Photograph of Sawo Island, Solomon Islands in the Pacific Ocean Michael Runkel, robertharding / Alamy Stock Photo

Fig 4 Dickens Rochester/Chatham Kind permission of David A Purdue. The Charles Dickens Page charlesdickenspage.com

Fig 5 Sphinx ligustri Privet moth, caterpillar and pupa drawn and engraved by Richard Nodder 1800 Florilegius /Alamy Photo Stock

Fig 6 Hoo sunrise, Isle of Grain 2014 David Lyon / Alamy Stock Photo

Fig 7 Corophium longicorne. Photographer Artokoloro, Penta Springs Limited /Alamy Stock Photo

Fig 8 Lino print of book 'Travels into the Interior Parts of Africa' by Jack Fawdry Tatham

CHAPTER TWO

Figure 9 St John's College Cambridge from the River Cam Photograph Kate Hooper

Fig 10 Statue of Adam Sedgwick, Museum of Earth Sciences, Cambridge Photographer Steve Vidler. Mauritius Images GmbH/Alamy Stock Photo

Fig 11 Ammonite found by Joe Hooper, Jurassic Coast, UK. Photograph Tim Hooper

Fig 12 Lecture Rooms of Botanic Garden, by kind permission from Dr Edwin Rose

Fig 13 Mount Vesuvius Steve Starbuck/ Alamy Stock Photo

Fig14 Lino print of Swimming Crab Polybius henslowii, Jack Fawdry Tatham

Fig 15 Etching of Setina irorella Photograph Kate Hooper

CHAPTER THREE

Fig 16 Henslow Teaching sheet on Primula officinalis, Cambridge University Herbarium

Fig 17 Abbe Rene Hauy, Science History Images / Alamy Stock Photo

Fig 18 Botanic Garden 1815 Drawn by W. Westall, Engraved by J. Sadler, by kind permission from Dr Edwin Rose

Fig 19 Thomas Martyn The History Collection / Alamy Stock Photo

Fig 20 Botanical illustration of Malvacaeae drawn by J S Henslow, Cambridge University Herbarium

Fig 21 Announcement of Botany Course, Cambridge University Herbarium

Fig 22 Wiliam Jackson Hooker, The Natural History Museum / Alamy Stock

Fig 23 John Lindley Old Paper Studios / Alamy Stock Photo

Fig 24 Joseph Hooker, Drawn by George Richmond 1835, Photo Researchers Science History Images / Alamy Stock Photos

Fig 25 Photograph of Main Entrance gate of Cambridge University Botanic Garden showing Trinity Hall coat of arms. Photograph Kate Hooper

Fig 26 Aerial photograph of Cambridge Systematic Beds. Kind permission of Howard Rice

Fig 27 Eschscholzia californica , William Hooker illustration, annotated by John Stevens Henslow. Cambridge University Herbarium

Fig 28 Queen Victoria, Prince Albert and their children. Niday Picture Library / Alamy Stock Photo

CHAPTER FOUR

Fig 29 Isaac Newton the Granger Collection / Alamy Stock Photo

Fig 29 Fossil of Irish Elk David Coleman Have Camera Will Travel / Alamy Stock Photo

Fig 30 Shells and fossils Photograph Kate Hooper

Fig 32 /33 /34 'Geological Survey of Anglesea' J S Henslow. Kind permission of the Cambridge Philosophical Society.

Fig 35 Herbarium sheet Moenchia erecta Cambridge University Herbarium

Fig 36 Herbarium sheet Juncus triglumis Cambridge University Herbarium

CHAPTER SIX

Fig 57 Lino print Henslow and Darwin on nature walk in Cambridgeshire Jack Fawdry Tatham

Fig 58 Lino print of Natter jack toad (Epidalea calamita). Jack Fawdry Tatham

Fig 59 The Beagle Classic Images / Alamy Stock Photo

Fig 60 Herbarium sheet Vulpia tenella, Cambridge University Herbarium

Fig 61 Herbarium sheet Opuntia galapageia, Cambridge University Herbarium

Fig 62 Illustration sheet Opuntia galapageia, Cambridge University Herbarium

Fig 63 Lino print Charles Darwin, a chimp and bird. Jack Fawdry Tatham

Fig 64 Lino print Henslow's sparrow Ammodramus henslowii. Kate Hooper

CHAPTER SEVEN

Fig 65 Harvest mice Lou Owen-Jones / Alamy Stock Photo

Fig 66 Lino print Camberwell Beauty. Jack Fawdry Tatham

Fig 67 Herbarium sheet Anagellis monelli, Cambridge University Herbarium

Fig 68 Family tree of John Stevens Henslow. Photograph Tim Hooper

Fig 69 Cover of Bouquet of Souvenirs. Constructed by Kate Hooper

Fig 70 Detail from herbarium sheet of Scolopendrium vulgare (Phyllitis scopopendrium) Cambridge University Herbarium

Fig 71 John Stevens Henslow in later life Alamy Stock Photo

FURTHER READING

1. Jenyns L Memoir of the Rev John Henslow London Van Voorst (1862)

2. Waters and Stowe, Darwin's Mentor (2001) Cambridge University Press

3. Walters, S. M The Shaping of Cambridge Botany (1981) Cambridge University Press

4. Russell- Gebbett, Jean, Henslow of Hitcham. Lavenham, Suffolk Terence Dalton (1977)

5. Henslow, George. John Stevens Henslow https://en.wikisource.org/wiki/Makers_of British botany/ John_Stevens_Henslow_1796-1861.

6. Pearn, Alison. Darwin All that matters. London John Murray Learning (2015)

7. Blythe, Ronald, Next to Nature, John Murphy (2022)

8. Darwin and his flowers. The Key to Natural Selection. Allan, Mea Faber and Faber, London (1977)

9. Darwin and Henslow: The Growth of an Idea (Letters 1831-1860) Edited by Nora Barlow. Murray 1967

10. Editor Nora Barlow, Autobiography of Charles Darwin. Collins (1958)

11. Clements, J. Darwin's Notebook The History Press (2009)

12. Browne, J. Charles Darwin Voyaging Vol 1 of a Biography London Jonathan Cape (1995)

13. Martin, Edward, Hitcham A Landscape, Social and Ecclesiastical History of a Suffolk Clayland Parish. Suffolk Archaeology and History (2021)

14. The Hitcham Millenium Book (2001)

15. Henslow, John Stevens Sketches on a course of lectures in Botany (1833)

16. Wheeler, Ian (Ed) Leonard Jenyns, Darwin's Lifelong Friend A Victorian Naturalist & his World. The Bath Royal Literary and Scientific Institute

17. Henslow, John Stevens, Le Bouquet des Souvenirs (1840)
18. Letters of Charles Darwin and John Stevens Henslow https://epsilon.ac.uk/
19. Kohn, Murrell, Parker and Whitehorn What Henslow taught Darwin Vol 436/4 Nature August 2005
20. Henslow, J.S A Catalogue of British Plants, (1829) Cambridge University Press
21. Parker, John, The Development of The Cambridge University Botanic Garden Curtis's Botanical Magazine 23 (Pt1) February (2006)
22. Henslow, J. S, Address to the Members of the University of Cambridge on the expediency of improving, and on the funds required for remodelling and supporting the Botanic Garden. Metcalfe and Palmer (Cambridge) (1846)
23. Henslow, J. S. Selected Papers 1821-38, Foreword by John S. Parker, Cambridge Library Collections, Cambridge University Press (2014)
24. Parker, John, Day S & Rose S. The Sainsbury Laboratory Science Architecture Art , Plant Science and the Origins of Cambridge Botanic Garden Black Dog Press (2011)
25. Knight, Frances. The Nineteenth Century Church and English Society. Cambridge University Press (1995)
26. Glover, Beverley, Directors Choice, Cambridge University Botanic Garden Scala Arts and Heritage Publishers Ltd. (2020)

Acknowledgements

Thank you Lisa Harris, Collection & Interpretation Manager, Food Museum, Stowmarket for letting me use the information from the display panels Walking with Henslow Exhibition, Food Museum 2020.

Thank you John Parker for letting me use his information from the display Darwin and Henslow Exhibition at Cambridge University Botanic Garden 2009.

Author Biography

After graduating from the Barts Medical College University of London in Medicine in 1985 Kate pursued a career in General Practice for over thirty-five years. She finally hung up the stethoscope after her first grandson was born.

Her love for Botany developed from the small patch of garden allocated to her aged five, to studying Garden Design at Writtle College and taking the Royal Horticultural Society's Certificate in Horticulture at the beginning of this Millenium. With Melanie Hanson, her business partner she designed many gardens as Perfect Circle Designs.

Kate has lived in the Cambridge area for over 30 years and she enjoys gardening with Tim, her husband, in the fine but dry East Anglian climate. They have three brilliant sons, three beautiful daughters-in-law, two gorgeous grandsons and are not all biased.

Kate was delighted to be accepted as a Volunteer Guide at the Cambridge Botanic Garden in 2022 and to become part of the volunteer team in the Herbarium in 2023. These two roles inspired her to find out more about Professor John Stevens Henslow who founded the Botanic Garden in its current site and who did so much to promote understanding of the natural world.

Artist Biography Jack Fawdry Tatham

Jack Fawdry Tatham is an artist based in the North West of England. Working primarily in the medium of printmaking his work focuses on the beauty of the natural world, often mixing imagined scenes with drawing from life. In 2024 he set up Market Place Print Studio in Cockermouth, Cumbria with his Parter Emily Baker, where they run art workshops as well as selling artwork and gifts made from the studio.